CONSTRUCTION INDUSTRY MANAGEMENT PRACTICES AND INNOVATION IN SMALL AND MEDIUM ENTERPRISES

AN EXPLORATORY QUALITATIVE STUDY

Blessing Okere, PhD

CONSTRUCTION INDUSTRY MANAGEMENT PRACTICES AND INNOVATION IN SMALL AND MEDIUM ENTERPRISES AN EXPLORATORY QUALITATIVE STUDY

iUniverse books may be ordered through booksellers or by contacting:

iUniverse
1663 Liberty Drive
Bloomington, IN 47403
www.iuniverse.com
844-349-9409

Because of the dynamic nature of the Internet, any web addresses or links contained in this book may have changed since publication and may no longer be valid. The views expressed in this work are solely those of the author and do not necessarily reflect the views of the publisher, and the publisher hereby disclaims any responsibility for them.

Any people depicted in stock imagery provided by Getty Images are models, and such images are being used for illustrative purposes only.
Certain stock imagery © Getty Images.

ISBN: 978-1-6632-0051-8 (sc)
ISBN: 978-1-6632-0052-5 (e)

Library of Congress Control Number: 2020917035

Print information available on the last page.

iUniverse rev. date: 09/14/2020

This work is dedicated to
the loving memory of my mother, Esther Nnenna Okere,
who provided a good foundation and instilled in me the attributes of
drive and persistence.

CONTENTS

LIST OF FIGURES

LIST OF TABLES

ACKNOWLEDGMENTS

My special thanks on this book go to my friends and colleagues who have supported me and contributed ideas developed in this book. My sincere appreciation goes to my mentor Dr. Cheryl McConnaughey at Capella University for her valuable contributions, and to Dr. Tony Pizur, Dr. Susan Miller, and Dr. Elaine Gregory for providing outstanding support and feedback on the original manuscript. A special word of thanks goes to Professor Pauline Eboh for her long-standing support and encouragement.

I also want to thank Dr. Camillus Njoku, Dr. Uzoma Uwakwe, Hon. Magistrate Victor Nwaeke, and Mr. James Odudu for their encouragement and contributions to this book. I am especially grateful to my aunt Julia Irrchukwu for her love and support throughout this process. My family provides indispensable support for all that I do: my dad, Aloysius, and my siblings, Kingsley, Chris, Kingdom, Joseph, Dominica, Gift, Justice, and Perpetual, thanks. Your selfless love and support are the motivation I use to push myself to do more and be more each day. My profound gratitude to you for the joy you all bring to my life.

CHAPTER 1

INTRODUCTION

Firms operate in a dynamic and uncertain business environment characterized by know-how and expertise to develop and implement products and services with superior value, including small- and medium-sized enterprises (SMEs) and the construction industry. Limited established management practices relate to SMEs in the construction industry. Limited research describes the relationship between management practices and innovation in the construction industry SMEs (Kamal, Yusof, and Iranmanesh 2016). The purpose of the qualitative research was to address the lack of existing knowledge about the relationship between management practices and innovation by exploring management practices used to advance innovation and business outcomes. SMEs in US organizations have fewer than five hundred workers (Gilmore et al. 2013). SMEs play an essential role in the US economy because they employ more than half the workforce in the private sector (Ilegbinosa and Jumbo 2015).

The construction industry is a multifaceted industry that requires management effort to engage in practices that create innovation. These management practices are the skills, knowledge, culture, and resources (Yusof et al. 2014) necessary to achieve successful innovation in the construction industry. Some management practices relate to how managers monitor general performance, how managers nurture the internal innovation climate, how managers ensure infrastructural and structural support for innovation is available to teams, and how managers reward risk-taking behaviors. An additional management practice identified in the literature points to the creation and implementation of new ideas to provide higher value to customers and other stakeholders and how companies embrace and experiment with new thoughts, including willingness to take risks and openness to inspiring new ideas (Moriano et al. 2014).

Innovation is an essential practice in the development and success of an organization (Jiménez-Jiménez and Sanz-Valle 2011; Tuan et al. 2016). Innovation is the foundation of a competitive edge when it creates a higher value for customers than rivals can do (Hamdani and Wirawan 2012). Partnership channels offer SMEs the opportunity to access skills, knowledge, and technology outside their core competency and to increase their capacity for sustainable innovation (Najib, Dewi, and Widyastuti 2014). Nurturing an internal innovation climate supports organizational readiness to innovate (Oke, Prajogo, and Jayaram 2013).

1

Background of the Study

Open innovation focuses on the development of in-house and outside resources to create significant value in the firm (Chesbrough 2006b). Open innovation offers a model of how organizations merge various modes to achieve open innovation (Chesbrough 2006b). This section provides a brief overview of the theoretical framework, SMEs, and the construction industry by evaluating the viability of SMEs in the construction industry using the theoretical application of open innovation.

The guiding theoretical framework for the research is open innovation theory (OIT; Abouzeedan and Hedner 2012; Chesbrough 2012; Crema, Verbano, and Venturini 2014; Hossain 2013; Storchevoi 2015). Given researchers' increasing interest in understanding the innovativeness of SMEs (Bouncken, Pesch, and Kraus 2015; Love and Roper 2015), the research goal was to bridge the gap between management practices and innovation by exploring the experiences of SME construction middle managers with management practices that may facilitate change. SMEs generate economic and social value because of their innovative capabilities (T. F. Chen 2012), but they fail to address management practices that lead to SME innovation in the construction industry.

OIT emphasizes the combination of internal and external expertise to advance innovation. OIT allows collaboration among external and internal groups in an organization (Chesbrough 2006a; Lichtenthaler 2011). An innovating firm can collaborate with competitors, suppliers, customers, research institutions, professional entities, and universities (Coras and Tantau 2013). The collaboration consists of collaborative innovation, innovation networks, and joint ventures. The ability to establish partnerships with outside organizations is essential for successful innovation in SMEs. The innovation process of some SMEs is ineffective and insufficient to encourage, support, and execute lucrative ideas that could enhance profits (Zakaria, Chew-Abdullah, and Yusoff 2016). The ability to resourcefully access expertise externally can yield better innovative results (Lasagni 2012).

An organization can collaborate with an external partner in innovation to alleviate the cost structure, share risk, pool resources, and augment the knowledge base (Coras and Tantau 2013). The growth of intellectual capital and knowledge acquisition attracts SMEs to collaborate and grow to be competitive (Lasagni 2012). Collaboration provides SMEs quick access to expertise that is beyond their reach internally. Partnerships boost the opportunity for SMEs to launch novel products and services successfully.

However, OIT can also challenge SMEs as it requires considerable organizational dedication to manage the information processes (Rogbeer, Almahendra, and Ambos 2014). Given that OIT entails an exchange of knowledge and expertise (Yoo, Sawyerr, and Tan 2015), SMEs risk collaboration failure, and for an organization to lose competitive edge supposes core expertise flows to rivals (Yoo et al. 2015). Firms must identify their innovation strategy and distinguish how research and development can support innovation goals (Pisano 2015). The lack of an innovation strategy makes implementing innovation extremely difficult as organizational members may perceive differing priorities (Pisano 2015). Setting clear goals, priorities, and plans, starting at the early stage of innovation, could help firms gain positive business results (Hilman and Kaliappen 2015; Standing and Kiniti 2011).

In recent years, attention tended to focus on the ability of organizations to expand their innovations (Saunila, Ukko, and Rantanen 2014). Scholars recognized SMEs as the driving force of economic growth (Gilmore et al. 2013; Karadag 2015; Mañez et al. 2013). Despite the economic relevance of SMEs, many SMEs still find it challenging to attain innovation that leads to growth and stability (Ajayi and Morton 2015). Developing SMEs' innovation ability has become of heightened interest and a major priority of SME managers to guarantee their continued existence and growth in the economy (Wonglimpiyarat 2015). Building on this interest, the study explored the perceptions and experiences of middle managers with management practices and innovation in the SME construction industry.

The scope of innovation in the construction industry is extensive and includes developing a new product, new materials, and new systems on construction know-how, equipment, and business operations (Goodland, Lindberg, and Shorthouse 2015). A review of the construction innovation literature indicates that the construction sector has a low-level investment in innovation (Shahbazpour, Noktehdan, and Wilkinson 2015). Nevertheless, the construction industry has numerous features that can improve the ability to implement innovation (Yusof et al. 2014). In the absence of market competition, change in the construction industry becomes an important task for managers to create an incentive to innovate (Shahbazpour et al. 2015). Regardless of the implications of innovation in achieving sustainable growth, most construction companies still experience a lack of innovation (Kamal et al. 2016; Yusof and Abidin 2011).

Innovation is a necessary source of growth for the construction industry, as it provides an opportunity to differentiate products or services (Kissi, Dainty, and Liu 2012). In the construction industry, innovation is determined by several elements. Examples include pursuing new business opportunities because of changes in economic conditions, developing solutions to address problems across the organization, aspiring to boost performance and profitability, and working to better respond to customer needs (Kissi et al. 2012). The construction industry centers innovation on the creation of products, services, and processes. Such products or services progress through the distribution channel to the marketplace, and methods involve cost reduction and enhanced quality (Kissi et al. 2012). Practices that enhance approaches to delivering products and improve processes are foundational to achieving objectives and meeting the needs of customers in the SME construction industry.

Rationale

A review of literature associated with management practices and innovation in SMEs in the construction industry led to the determination that a gap exists in the body of work related to construction industry management practices and innovation in SMEs. Extensive research abounds related to the construction industry (Shahbazpour et al. 2015; Yusof et al. 2014); however, scant information emerged specifically to management practices and innovation in SMEs in the construction industry.

The research is significant to the field of business management because SMEs are an integral part of the overall economy and innovation is a primary driver in the ability of SMEs to flourish. The study aimed to determine the relationship between management practices and innovation in SMEs in the US construction industry. The findings could improve the innovation capabilities of SMEs in the construction industry. The study also aimed to ascertain the essential part that SMEs play in the economy and innovation. SMEs have a positive influence in the United States on the nonfarm private gross domestic product (GDP) and hold a supportive role in new employment in the economy (Ilegbinosa and Jumbo 2015).

Also, limited research examined how OIT may relate to the use of management practices that may contribute to innovation in SMEs in the construction industry. OIT allows firms to collaborate with competitors, customers, suppliers, professional institutions, and research laboratories (Coras and Tantau 2013). However, scant knowledge exists on the relationship of management practices to innovation in construction industry SMEs. The research results may help middle managers perform responsibilities associated with innovation successfully. The study may also contribute to the experience of SME construction industry middle managers who have implemented practices that improved innovation in their organizations and may provide additional information about middle management practices and innovation that support sustainable growth in SMEs in the construction industry.

Purpose of the Study

The purpose of the exploratory qualitative research was to add to the existing literature on management practices by exploring the constructs of OIT to determine how middle manager practices facilitate innovations in SMEs in the construction industry.

The primary constructs of OIT consist of collaborative innovation and innovation networks. The research entailed investigating the link between management practices and innovation in SMEs because SMEs are significant to economic growth (Karadag 2015). The knowledge gathered on how different management practices may lead to real value creation can help facilitate the growth of SMEs in the construction industry.

Despite the growing interest in OIT research, thoughts on OIT in SMEs have been inadequate in mainstream research (Wynarczyk 2013), as researching smaller organizations seems more challenging than in larger organizations. Because of limited resources for innovation, the need to launch improved products and share risks allied with innovation creation has necessitated SMEs collaborating with partners and networks to innovate (Wagner 2012). Collaboration with other firms that aim at innovation could facilitate an exchange of knowledge, information, and experiences, thereby improving how organizations learn and work (Malmström Wincent, and Johansson 2013). Collaboration with partners allows the transfer of explicit and tacit knowledge, which facilitates the generation of innovation (Azadegan 2011; Wagner 2012).

Significance of the Study

SMEs are the driving force of economic growth (Gilmore et al. 2013; Karadag 2015; Mañez et al. 2013). Despite the economic relevance of SMEs, many SME organizations still find it challenging to attain innovation that leads to growth and stability (Ajayi and Morton 2015). Innovation is necessary for firms to compete successfully and achieve a competitive advantage (Arlbjørn and Paulraj 2013).

Significance to Scholars

The study filled the gap in the existing body of research related to management practices and innovation in the construction sector. The current qualitative exploratory study is significant in that it enabled exploration of the constructs of OIT to establish middle managers' practices that facilitate innovation in the construction industry SMEs. The research is significant in that it provides an alternate method of study for OIT with management practices and innovation in the construction industry SMEs in the absence of quantitative and empirical research.

Significance to Practitioners

The study is significant in providing viable information about management practices and innovation for practitioners. Particularly, middle managers in the construction industry SMEs may benefit from the insights. Data from the study could inform middle managers, practitioners, and SMEs that are considering initiating innovation development.

Significance to Organizations

Construction industry SMEs not only need to depend on internal capabilities as a source of innovation but also must rely on the competencies of their innovation collaborators and networks to innovate. By learning more about the management practices used by construction industry SMEs when working to innovate, those in management positions may determine how to promote innovation, compete, and flourish. The study is viable in enabling the insight of management practices as critical to completing innovation in the construction industry SMEs.

Research Question

The research explored the relationship between management practices and innovation in SMEs in the construction industry. The following research question guided the study: What roles do management practices have in innovation in US SMEs in the construction industry?

Definition of Terms

The following descriptions are presented to elucidate the terminology used in the research:

Construction industry. Firms that are project-based and of a short-term nature (Segerstedt and Olofsson 2010). Participants indicated they worked in the construction industry when screened for study participation.

Innovation. Something improved or new that presents real value to consumers (Stroh 2015). Participants self-reported innovation during study interviews.

Management practices. Those activities undertaken by management (al-Sehaimi, Patricia, and Koskela 2014). Participants self-reported management practices during study interviews.

Middle managers. Individuals over low-supervision positions and under top management who are responsible for strategic decisions, for example, senior managers or directors in various business units (Kissi et al. 2012). Participants indicated they were middle managers in answer to screening questions for participation in the research.

Small- and medium-sized enterprises (SMEs). SMEs are independent businesses with fewer than five hundred employees (Gilmore et al. 2013). Participants indicated they worked for a firm that has fewer than five hundred employees in answer to screening questions for participation in the study.

Research Design

A qualitative exploratory method was used for the study to determine how middle managers in SMEs in the construction industry, through management practices, contribute to innovation. An exploratory research inquiry is a viable approach to study individuals' personal beliefs and experiences. Exploratory qualitative inquiry examines people's experiences. Building blocks for exploratory qualitative research include defining the qualitative question, gathering prior knowledge, and possessing the desire to understand the point of view of participants (Percy, Kostere, and Kostere 2015). Researchers use exploratory qualitative inquiry to learn more about how individuals allot meaning to social or human reality and use the individual's words to describe phenomena studied (Collins and Cooper 2014; Hickson 2011). Researchers collect participant perceptions from their worldview perspectives and lived experiences (Allwood 2012).

The exploratory qualitative inquiry allowed data collection of subjective opinions of middle managers in the construction industry and explores emerging fields, management practices, and innovation. Researchers use qualitative designs to examine subjective opinions (Percy et al. 2015). Qualitative inquiry addresses ambiguous phenomena and provides valuable proof from lived experience (Birchall 2014). The qualitative research methodology employs inductive reasoning, allowing an adaptable method from which a researcher may conclude data and analysis, conducted as the study develops (Locke 2011). An inductive rationale focuses on the researcher to investigate and construct meaning as findings surface from the data (Locke 2011).

Because of the nature of the study, the qualitative exploratory inquiry was used to discover the complexity of middle managers' experiences in the construction industry SMEs regarding innovation practices. Semistructured interviews were used to collect data for the research study. A semistructured interview is a valuable form of data collection (Baumbusch 2010), used broadly in qualitative studies for data collection, allowing a researcher to rephrase questions more efficiently to suit participants' understanding rather than adhering to predetermined questions (Allwood 2012). Semistructured interviews allow participants to share their experiences through guided questions (Percy et al. 2015). Results from the data collection provided a guideline of management practices and innovation that supports sustainable growth of the construction industry SMEs in the United States.

Assumptions and Limitations

Qualitative research has related assumptions and limitations. Assumptions are the fundamental drivers of studies, enabling a researcher to recognize aspects of the research to neglect (Leedy and Ormrod 2010). Limited analysis relates to weakness in research (Pajares 2007). Delimitations include items overlooked in a study (Pajares 2007). This section provides a discussion of the assumptions, limitations, and delimitations related to the study.

Assumptions

The study has assumed relevance to practitioners and academics. No deliberate bias or researcher error was assumed to intrude into the study. It was assumed that the study was conducted in a controlled manner to ensure credibility, avoidance of risks, confidentiality, privacy, and security of data. Assumptions for the study included methodological, theoretical, and topical as indicated.

General methodological assumptions. Methodological assumptions included the ontology, epistemology, and axiology focus of the study. Ontology addresses concerns about reality (real-life experience), distinct from other things (Converse 2012). Facts are independent of another person's reality. Participants experience the study phenomenon differently because their real-life experiences are independent of the life experiences of others. It was assumed the participants' responses during the interviews were honest and that their experiences differed, although they may have had commonalities in their experiences.

Epistemology concerns knowledge that answers the question of what can be known and who can know it (Converse 2012). It was assumed that adequate efforts were made to control biases toward, judgment of, and personal experience with the study topic. Participants' experiences were the focus of the inquiry, which required engagement in mindfulness meditation. Mindfulness means consistent awareness and nonjudgmental experiences (Davis and Hayes 2011).

Axiology is the importance of value in research (Grill 2017). It was assumed that the study findings would show the perceptions and experiences of middle managers regarding management practices and innovation. The researcher tried not to bring any specific values to the study. It was assumed the use of a journal would help check biases and prevent them from tainting the integrity of the investigation and study findings. It was also assumed that an exploratory qualitative study would not consider reality to be linear and that experiences would accrue from interviews with participants.

Theoretical assumptions. OIT was assumed to be the appropriate theoretical choice for the study. It was assumed this would provide viable knowledge about the use of management practices to define innovation processes in SMEs in the construction industry. SMEs generate economic and social value because of their innovative capabilities (T. F. Chen 2012). A clearly defined innovation line leads to the sustainable growth of innovation (Engel et al. 2015).

Topic-specific assumptions. It was assumed that management practices could improve innovation and business outcomes (Bossink 2007; Ofori-Boadu et al. 2012). Implementing effective management practices could increase the capacity of a firm to achieve project results (P. Chen, Qiang, and Wang 2009). Management practices could be classified through Malcolm Baldrige National Quality Improvement Act criteria such as knowledge management, strategic planning, leadership, measurement and analysis, customer focus, operation, and workforce focus (Ofori-Boadu et al. 2012). The level of success achieved in implementing technological innovation depends on management practices, resources, and processes used for the implementation (Ofori-Boadu et al. 2012).

Limitations

In researching the relationship between management practices and innovation, study limitations relate to the population study size and sampling. Limited sample size and the inability to generalize study results both limit the ability to make generalizable industry recommendations (Goffin et al. 2012) and may not accurately reflect every SME in the construction industry. Qualitative researchers frequently state sample size in qualitative research, but the center of the discussion is always simplistic and, to some extent, uninformed (Boddy 2016). Qualitative research lacks the justification for sample sizes in research (Boddy 2016; Marshall et al. 2013).

Design flaw limitations. A research design limitation was that the findings could not be statistically generalized. The study was limited to middle managers who have three or more years of working experience in SMEs in the construction industry. Another limitation was that the study focused on the role of management practices on innovation. Snowball sampling also limited the study. Last, being new to the qualitative process, the researcher had the limitation of lack of experience in conducting qualitative research.

Delimitations. One study delimitation was that strategic innovation processes not supported by management practices were not studied. Senior management positions and first-level management positions were also not studied factors. Construction industry innovation classification processes were not investigated. An analysis of the data using demographic information was not conducted. These areas were beyond the scope of the study, given the focus on determining relationships between management practices and innovation in the construction industry SMEs.

Organization of the Remainder of the Study

The remainder of the study consists of four chapters. Chapter 2 includes a review of the literature with a detailed theoretical framework description, the construction industry, SMEs, innovation, OIT, open innovation in SMEs, management practices, and middle managers. Also contained in chapter 2 are syntheses of the research findings in existing literature and a critique of previous research related to the current study topic. Chapter 3 presents the research design, sample, data collection, data analysis, interview protocol, and ethical considerations. Chapter 4 addresses the data analysis and research findings, including a description of participants and a summary. Chapter 5 presents a discussion of the research findings, conclusions, a comparison of results to previous literature, interpretation of study findings, implications, and recommendations for future research.

CHAPTER 2

LITERATURE REVIEW

The focus of this work was to explore the relationship between management practices and innovation in US SMEs in the construction industry. Three themes and concepts in the literature review, investigated in support of the study, included (a) OIT, open innovation performance, open innovation opportunities, and internal innovation climate; (b) SME, open innovation in SMEs; and (c) construction industry SMEs, middle managers in the construction industry, and management practices in the construction industry. This chapter includes a discussion of the conceptual framework for the study. Chapter 2 also offers a review of current research, methodologies used, and a critique of previous research related to the topic. The literature review section consists of three parts, an examination OIT, the scholarly literature on SMEs and open innovation in SMEs, and content related to the construction industry, including a discussion of academic research on innovation in the construction industry, and middle managers and management practices in the construction industry.

Methods of Searching

The main reason a researcher conducts a review of the literature on a topic of interest is to extract the existing body of research in that area (Blank, Rokach, and Shani 2016; Hinde and Spackman 2015). Conducting such a review may not require a stipulated pattern to follow. Some researchers provide guidelines on planning and designing scholarly research. These guidelines include identifying relevant keywords, databases, and search engines (Blank et al. 2016; Su, Hsu, and Pai 2010). When reviewing the abstracts of previous research on the related topic, researchers seek keywords. Obtaining a high recall of keywords requires analysis of the other sections (Shah et al. 2003). Nevertheless, no consensus exists on a method for selecting keywords (Blank et al. 2016).

To locate relevant information and journal articles associated with the study topic of construction industry management practices and innovation, the guidance of Blank et al. (2016) and Su et al. (2010) was followed. The following key terms were used: *construction industry, small and medium enterprises, innovation, construction industry innovation, SMEs innovation, innovation benefits, innovation challenges, innovation strategy, construction industry management practices,* and *innovation development in the construction industry.* Other search terms included *middle managers in construction industry, middle managers innovation practices, middle managers and innovation, the role of middle managers and innovation management, open innovation theory, open innovation construct, managing collaboration, collaborative innovation,* and *network innovation.*

Additional search terms included *knowledge flow, internal innovation in SMEs, internal innovation in the construction industry, internal and external,* and *innovation in SME construction industry.* Also, search terms included *capturing outside ideas, openness to open innovation, benefits of open innovation in the construction industry, benefits of open innovation in SMEs, open innovation strategy, challenges and limitations of open innovation, challenges and opportunities in open innovation, internal innovation climate,* and *innovation culture.* After identifying key terms needed to locate pertinent information and journal articles related to the study topic, research questions, and theory that informed the research, additional specific databases were explored.

Identifying sources related to the research topic was a significant step in the research. After establishing the research topic, the scope narrowed to focus on earlier works and the recent body of research that addresses the research problem. A review of the literature was initiated by searching and classifying articles associated with the research topic. Some researchers indicated that when searching for items, it would be best to search for articles in a particular area (Blank et al. 2016; Su et al. 2010). In this context, keywords provided a significant advantage in identifying articles relevant to the current study.

In my conducting a review of the available literature on the topic under study, Capella University's library was employed to access primary resources in multiple scholarly works of research, journal databases, and related bodies of work on the topic: construction industry management practices and innovation. The review process entailed searching for keywords while using controlled vocabulary and using the authors' names. The most frequently used search engine was Summon because of its ability to extend searches across Capella's library collections for journal articles, dissertations, and books, and because such searches are easily narrowed by topic and year of publication.

In carrying out the literature review, a combination of search terms was used to obtain relevant information. Examples include Boolean search keywords with operators *and, not,* and *or* (Adorno, Garbee, and Marix 2016). Using this search method yielded relevant articles as searches focused on materials related to the topic under study

(Blank et al. 2016; Hinde and Spackman 2015). Keywords related to qualitative research methods, such as qualitative inquiry, qualitative approach, exploratory, empirical case studies, ethnography, grounded theory, and phenomenology.

Additionally, the literature review taxonomy was followed as described by Collins and Cooper (2014). The taxonomy includes an orderly categorized literature search centered on focus goal, coverage, and organization. The focus could be on the study methods and practices (al-Maian et al. 2015). In such cases, the center was on management practices and innovation discussed in the literature review. A literature review synthesizes the literature on the research topic in a way that generates new perspectives or frameworks (al-Maian et al. 2015). In this review of writing, the goal was to attain a literature review that supported or made new ideas regarding construction industry management practices and innovation in SMEs. The coverage of the literature relates to the significant aspect of the literature focus and goal (al-Maian et al. 2015). Three primary areas of the research were a review of the literature conducted in OIT, SMEs, and the construction industry body of work. The limitation of the literature review relates to the notion that the focus and research goal build on OIT, SMEs, and construction industry management practices. The body of work on management practices and innovation related to SMEs and the construction industry was also explored.

Furthermore, a literature review was conducted using various databases, including ABI/INFORM Collection, Google Scholar, and Business Source Complete. The selection criteria centered on peer-reviewed and scholarly publications. Articles were selected after reviewing abstracts and their relevance to the topic identified and evaluated in detail to ensure they added new knowledge to the area of study. Additional relevant documents from the references lists of articles and dissertations were also part of the literature review. In addition to other databases was Dissertation @ Capella, which contains full-text coverage for most dissertations written by Capella University graduates.

Conceptual Framework for the Study

In the study, the emerging body of work on management practices and innovation using an exploratory qualitative inquiry was reviewed to investigate the relationship between management practices and innovation. Exploratory qualitative inquiry is an examination of people's experience as they reflect on external aspects of their lives (Percy et al. 2015). A qualitative approach addresses ambiguous phenomena and provides valuable proof from lived experience (Birchall 2014). The goal of a qualitative researcher is to obtain some general insight into a phenomenon (Andermause et al. 2017; Dowling, Lloyd, and Suchet-Pearson 2016; Housley et al. 2017).

The qualitative research methodology employs inductive reasoning, allowing for a flexible method to draw conclusions from data and analysis as the study develops (Locke 2011). Inductive reasoning focuses on the intention to investigate and construct meaning from the data as findings surface (Soltanifar and Ansari 2016). A qualitative researcher seeks to understand how individuals allot meaning to social or human reality and to use the individuals' words to describe the phenomena under investigation (Collins and Cooper 2014; Hickson 2011). It helps a researcher to perceive research participants from their worldview perspective and lived experiences (Allwood 2012). The inductive nature of the qualitative method allows a researcher to sharpen the research questions (Thompson 2017). A qualitative research method provides various means to obtain relevant information that is less appropriate for statistical quantification.

Semistructured interviews were a technique used in the study as they helped reveal essential facts regarding the topic under investigation as supported by Mojtahed, Nunes, Martins, and Peng (2014). The semistructured interview technique supports the conversational flow of information between the researcher and study participants, providing access to additional information and participants the chance to freely share their experiences (Mojtahed et al. 2014). An interpretative analysis was used to determine the relationship between theoretical concepts and specific topics that emerged from participants' responses. The interpretative analysis helped provide an awareness of how study participants described their experiences (Back, Gustafsson, and Berterö 2014). Two distinct epistemologies—positivism and constructivism—characterize the ways researchers conduct their studies. Qualitative methods of research align with the interpretive paradigm (Glesne 1999). The methodological process for the study focused on the philosophical beliefs of the nature of reality, value, and knowledge using a theoretical framework that enriched the conduct and interpretation of the research (Glesne 1999).

Review of the Literature

The literature review referenced literature on the implementation and success of management practices in construction industry SMEs. Management practices involve activities undertaken by management (al-Sehaimi et al. 2014). In essence, management practices drive progress, growth, and success in an organization, allowing managers to perform operations to achieve a common objective. The concept of management practices was explored to unveil construction industry management practices that are not being used and are untapped. Management practices have the potential to improve innovation and business outcomes through the activities of managers (al-Sehaimi et al. 2014).

An investigation of OIT and the degree to which it relates to SMEs and the construction industry in current literature is included in the literature review. Basic theoretical constructs and research findings are presented as the basis for further research on management practices and innovation. This section includes a review of OIT in conjunction with SMEs and the construction industry.

Open Innovation Theory

Various theoretical examinations of open innovation revealed that broader-framework settings influence OIT and that open innovation encompasses activities such as search, sourcing, cooperation, and licensing (Herstad et al. 2008). Some scholars claimed that the new era of OIT emerged as purposeful corporate practices whereby in-house investments on research and development were supplemented or substituted because of the extensive use of outside knowledge sourcing and outside involvement in commercialization (Herstad et al. 2008; Lazonick 2007). OIT emerged from technologies, growing knowledge flows, and information flows through rapid development and diffusion of digital information systems (Herstad et al. 2008). OIT creates elevated opportunities for first-mover advantage related to new product and service designs and levels of distribution of industrious competencies across organization boundaries (Chesbrough 2006c; Herstad et al. 2008).

Outside-in open innovation and inside-out open innovation. The two core forms of open innovation are outside in and inside out (Chesbrough 2006c, 2012, 2017). The overall categorization of outside in and inside out is a mix of inbound and outbound knowledge transfer (Enkel, Gassmann, and Chesbrough 2009). The outside-in form of open innovation involves the ability of firms to extend their innovation process by including external ideas and contributions, using outside ideas and know-how in their own businesses (Chesbrough 2006c; Gianiodis, Ettlie, and Urbina 2014). The outside-in open innovation has drawn attention from scholars and industries (Chesbrough 2012, 2017). Outside-in innovation focuses on the model in practice and the level of collaboration between various stakeholders (Inauen and Schenker-Wicki 2011). Outside-in open innovation is how companies source, screen, assess, attain, and leverage outside knowledge resources for their innovation practices (Dahlander and Gann 2010).

In contrast, companies involved in outside-in open innovation might desert the development of essential know-how competencies internally (Vanhaverbeke 2013). Outside-in innovation may increase companies' reliance on external partners

(Vanhaverbeke 2013). Firms involved in outside-in open innovations could face a high risk of competition in the market as externalizing critical knowledge seems to advance the strength of competition. These risks are problematic mainly for SMEs more so than for larger organizations (Spithoven, Vanhaverbeke, and Roijakkers 2013). Firms should not strictly engage in outside-in open innovation because of the high risks involved.

Through inside-out open innovation, companies systematically externalize their internal ideas and expertise (Chesbrough 2017; Dahlander and Gann 2010). Inside-out open innovation requires firms to allow unemployed and underused ideas to be accessible to other organizations (Chesbrough 2012). Unlike outside-in innovation, inside-out innovation is less engaged in academic research or industry practice (Chesbrough 2012, 2017).

Open innovation has profoundly influenced the trend in innovation research and practice (Fu 2012). Researchers explored open innovation and how it affects the firm's performance (Chesbrough 2006c; Dahlander and Gann 2010; Rahman and Ramos 2013). Researchers also investigated open innovation as a source of improving innovation performance, determined through the level of patents or innovative sales (Chiang and Hung 2010; Lee et al. 2010; Rohrbeck, Hölzle, and Gemünden 2009).

Drivers of open innovation theory. OIT emerged in the 1950s. It was expanded and consolidated in the 1960s, when vertically integrated mass production was common, resulting in the first generation of research and development organization (Roussel, Saad, and Erickson 1991; Vanhaverbeke and Cloodt 2006). The 1950s and 1960s marked an era of specialization and autonomy in research and development (Lam 2000). Quite early in the twentieth century, US industrial organizations collaborated and sourced research and development services from outside research and development laboratories (Vanhaverbeke and Cloodt 2006). Also, the early twentieth century was an era when new learning came with cartels and coordination connected to commerce relations, widespread and essential for overall progress and growth of the industrial structure, which was mostly controlled by small companies (Vanhaverbeke and Cloodt 2006).

Conditions necessary to the expansion of the regime were, among other things, the fast-growing local markets associated with massive incentives for businesses and organizations to invest in research and development, and the ongoing domination of organizations' decision makers who functioned independently. And, many believed, antitrust legislation led to the closure of vertical integration (Vanhaverbeke and Cloodt 2006). The economic downturn in the 1970s was very challenging to the regime, whereas in the 1980s the marketplace dissemination introduced product and service diversification and paved the way for best practices in companies and industries that operated outside the United States (Vanhaverbeke and Cloodt 2006). The organizations that worked outside the United States were the Marshallian industrial districts in Germany and Italy, that is, the network of collocated SMEs (Asheim and Isaksen 1997; Vanhaverbeke and Cloodt 2006). Industrial firms supported the transition from large organizations to smaller organizations (Piore and Sabel 1984), thereby expanding the method used to develop production and innovation (Vanhaverbeke and Cloodt 2006).

In the 1990s, various innovation practices gained much influence and formed the foundation for firms' investments in innovation and policy improvement. The growing attention to external resources was enhanced through research, and concepts developed in various companies, resulting from the focus on extended organizations, collaboration incentives (Dyer 2000), virtual organizations (Chesbrough and Teece 1996, 2002), and useful partnerships and collaboration of firms beyond boundaries (Helper 2000; Vanhaverbeke and Cloodt 2006). Following was a transition to the initial generation of research and development industries through the transitional marketplace, which moved to the next generation model, generating research and development firms. The progress of innovation led to the integration of internal research and development with other knowledge communities inside and outside the organization (Vanhaverbeke and Cloodt 2006). Innovation efforts were intended to highlight long-term organization planning and strategy and generate more portfolios of innovation projects with internal complementarities to facilitate the sharing of knowledge from various sources internally and support the sourcing of knowledge externally. The idea of learning organizations merged through an emphasis on processes, policies, and learning organizations as sustaining infrastructures.

The new era of open innovation theory. Recent studies referenced open innovation as distributed novel practices focused on the flow of knowledge, such as accessing, harnessing, and absorbing the flow of knowledge beyond companies' boundaries (Chesbrough 2017; West and Bogers 2017). Open innovation provided novel concepts such as the innovation funnel, product improvement and development, and business model changes in large organizations (Rodríguez-Ferradas and Alfaro-Tanco 2016). Open innovation was designed to support a firm's ability to collaborate with other firms in a meaningful way (Chesbrough 2017). The phenomenon supported organizations like Procter & Gamble to customize the crisps by printing text and images directly on Pringles chips, Italian bakeries with their edible ink, or the marketing of the Swiffer Duster through a licensing agreement with a Japanese firm already marketing the product (Chesbrough 2017). Open innovation supported Dell and IBM, reducing their research and development budgets and their dependence on partners to manage their product design and development (Azadegan 2011).

Changes in the business environment obliged firms to attain high-technology innovation through external knowledge, which has become critical to a firm's progress and growth (Crema et al. 2014). Organizations' ability to create knowledge internally may be insufficient, requiring reliance on external knowledge (Bauer and Leker 2013; Karamanos 2015; C. Wang et al. 2014) because of limited resources. External knowledge may be made available through open innovation, which is valuable for generating new knowledge. Open innovation has turned into a growing propensity of companies working beyond their boundaries of operation (Mina, Bascavusoglu-Moreau, and Hughes 2014).

Open innovation capability has expanded and incorporated novel ideas and models such as business model innovation and service innovation in contexts that combine multiple collaborating communities and ecosystems (Chesbrough 2017). Many organizations have transited from closed to open innovation because of external collaborations (Rodríguez-Ferradas and Alfaro-Tanco 2016). Companies have applied open innovation to different situations, and not only to new product development. Open innovation has connected to new product innovation and process innovation (Greco, Grimaldi, and Cricelli 2015) and has expanded beyond innovation indicators to include customer performance and financial performance (Mazzola, Bruccoleri, and Perrone 2016).

Moreover, open innovation focuses on the combination of internal and external viewpoints into platforms and systems that accelerate the inflow and outflow of expertise to grow inside innovation and expand markets for outside innovation (Chesbrough 2012). Open innovation primarily focuses on the integration of a firm's resources and capabilities from internal and external levels (Inauen and Schenker-Wicki 2011). Open innovation uses business models, strategies, and processes to outline the use of platforms and systems (Chesbrough 2012). These business models use inside and outside expertise to develop real value, using inside means to create such value (Chesbrough 2012).

Collaboration innovation. Open innovation models the possibility of collaboration and intersection in organizations. Collaboration, on the one hand, references a process by which individuals or firms with different expertise attain common objectives they cannot achieve independently (Kumar and Banerjee 2012). Intersection, in contrast, references a firm's ability to seek innovative ideas beyond the organization's boundaries (Abreu, Macedo, and Camarinha-Matos 2009). Innovators could use open innovation when the vertical integration perspective and the results from managing technology seem not to support a company's growth (Storchevoi 2015). In that case, a firm should change to a system of extensive know-how whereby key innovators play a central role in the innovation practice and are compensated for their contributions (Storchevoi 2015). The individual company completes the remaining work, creating any product of its own choice using the already provided extensive know-how. Companies in this situation have two options: the first is for the central company to generate expertise and take it to the individual company's innovators; the second is for key innovators to purchase the design from the innovating company and incorporate the know-how into their product (Storchevoi 2015).

Also, a firm can improve internal knowledge through alliance while maintaining know-how. Joint venture capabilities for alliance could be a useful means to improve innovation (Bos 2012). Alliance partners' know-how increases the exploration of innovation (Phelps 2010). OIT helps managers draw on external knowledge to augment internal knowledge, showing the importance of networking and of access to diverse ideas in a company's alliance formation (Phelps 2010). Allying with firms that have expertise in areas an organization cares about is of immense importance to such organizations.

Research on open innovation. Fast-growing interest in open innovation has become highly referenced in the literature (West and Bogers 2017). Dahlander and Gann's (2010) appraisal on open innovation shows a two-by-two framework of inbound (sourcing and acquiring) and outbound (revealing and selling) ideas, including innovation, describing a three-phase model of obtaining, integrating, and commercializing external innovations (West and Bogers 2014). Other reviews showed a prospective research agenda related to open innovation (Randhawa, Wilden, and Hohberger 2016; Tucci et al. 2016; West, Salter, et al. 2014).

Successful open innovation from external sources involves finding external sources of innovation and conveying the innovation to the organization (West and Bogers 2014). Researchers established different guidelines on how to obtain innovation through external resources. Dahlander and Gann (2010) identified the difference between monetary and nonmonetary inflow of innovation. Extant research on developing innovation from outside sources, formerly based in big firms in technological sectors, focuses on low-technological industries (Barge-Gil 2010; Grimpe and Sofka 2009; Lee et al. 2010; Spithoven, Clarysse, and Knockaert 2011; West and Bogers 2014). Organizations can generate innovation, knowledge, technological development, market expertise, and helpful resources to support innovation (Bogers and West 2012).

Measures of open innovation performance include product performance, new product release, innovative sales, and revenue growth (West and Bogers 2017). Nevertheless, researchers who focus on performance, sales, and growth fail to consider value capture, which includes effectiveness and efficiency, and the resultant aspects of innovation (West and Bogers 2014, 2017). Moreover, organizations need to address the open innovation performance of various forms across organization levels, demonstrated by the recent body of work on open innovation at the product level (Du, Leten, and Vanhaverbeke 2014; West and Bogers 2017).

Over the past fourteen years, most existing research emphasized the need to understand the conditions in which open innovation works. West and Bogers (2014) suggested acknowledging and understanding when open innovation does not work. Chesbrough and Brunswicker (2014) stated that more research is needed on these unstudied issues when firms abandon open innovation. Chesbrough (2006b, 2006c) established that the fundamental question of open innovation involves consideration of the false negative and false positive in innovation practices. Few research studies are concerned with these issues, although companies have much to gain from getting the whole picture of the exact antecedents of open innovation processes (West and Bogers 2017).

Challenges and limitations of open innovation. Open innovation efforts face challenges despite their offer to strengthen a firm's innovation performance and boost revenue (Chesbrough 2017). A significant problem relates to managing the effect of open innovation on inside innovation processes and the transfer of innovation results in the organization (Chesbrough 2017). Outside-in open innovation brings new ideas, but if the firm has not set up the downstream capacity to process these ideas, bottlenecks may slow the entire innovation process of the firm (Chesbrough 2017). Chesbrough (2017) advised linking the front end of open innovation to the back-end business to transfer innovation results to the market. A firm's open innovation efforts might be challenged by the limited ability of the lead developer to control the technological process of the project when working on a joint innovation project (Almirall and Casadesus-Masanell 2010). Another challenge is the synergistic gains expected in open innovation, where collaboration must be adequate to offset any incremental costs and losses associated with elevated levels of cooperation and coordination with partners (Almirall and Casadesus-Masanell 2010).

Open innovation is not without limitations. Open innovation puts a firm's intellectual property rights at risk if those rights are not adequately secured legally (Almirall and Casadesus-Masanell 2010). Most protection of intellectual property is not sufficient because trade secrets and proprietary knowledge are often vulnerable to unintended spillover to rivals (Yoo et al. 2015). In open innovation, the collaborating organization may have conflicting objectives (Almirall and Casadesus-Masanell 2010), or the goals of the partnering organization may not align perfectly because of the organization's intent to gain the most benefit (Almirall and Casadesus-Masanell 2010). A successful open innovation practice develops when it aligns with corporate strategy (Vanhaverbeke 2013). Companies should not limit their innovation investments to outside-in or inside-out open innovation as both can be viable practices in certain situations.

Another limitation of open innovation may be the workforce. Workers in some large organizations may not freely share knowledge, given their attitude toward job security and competition on a functional level or the individual worker level (Brunold and Durst 2012). The absence of trust between collaborating firms can threaten a collaboration effort that is essential to firms' success. Organizations must seek ways to prevent the risk of knowledge sharing to elevate competitiveness while considering open innovation. Sharing external knowledge could render an organization's core competencies accessible to its competitors (Lichtenthaler 2011). Consequently, a company could forfeit its competitive advantage by sharing knowledge. Also, sharing expertise could offer the competing organization additional benefits if it uses the shared experience to gain considerable market share (Lichtenthaler 2011).

Strengths of open innovation. Regardless of the challenges and limitations of open innovation, most researchers still promote it. Open innovation practices permit firms to merge internal and external resources, concepts, and know-how and allow them to benefit from both channels through collaboration with other firms (Wynarczyk 2013). Practices of open innovation are a powerful means of product diversity and discovery (Chesbrough 2006b). These practices create synergies between collaborators as the collaborators share knowledge that leads to innovation, which may not have happened inside a firm (Chesbrough 2017). Open innovation offers a higher value to firms in developing and marketing their technologies, thereby improving their expertise to innovate and gain competitiveness (Manceau et al. 2012; Petrariu, Bumbac, and Ciobanu 2013). Open innovation practice imitates competition between external and internal resources, increases the productivity of the collaborating organizations, and improves the quality of the work process in those organizations (Chesbrough 2006b).

Open innovation offers an economic advantage for companies, mainly in difficult economic times (Chesbrough 2006a). Open innovation is an approach that companies can successfully use to diminish noncore improvement efforts in difficult economic times if focused on critical businesses. The approach benefits firms that use the intellectual capital developed by other firms, thereby helping with innovations developed by others (Lichtenthaler 2011).

Innovation. The concept of innovation developed based on competition and strategies used by firms to compete (Azis, Darun, et al. 2017). Innovation is an invention of ideas, technologies, or processes or a way of improving products or services that help meet a particular need (Rahman and Ramos 2013). Innovation is a process of developing and implementing something new (Anderson, Potočnik, and Zhou 2014). *New* regarding innovation implies newness or novelty, not necessarily originality (Bergendahl and Magnusson 2015). Innovation creates a unique value that customers can identify. The innovativeness of an organization is what measures its ability to develop and implement new products and technology processes (Story, Boso, and Cadogan 2015). Something is innovative only when it adds value to the existing work process, policies, products, and services for the organization and consumers (Müller, Rammer, and Trüby 2009).

Innovation plays a decisive role in a company's ability to compete and to obtain a sustainable competitive advantage (Arlbjørn and Paulraj 2013; Azis and Osada 2010). Innovation creates value by driving economic growth, acting as an economic driving force, and offering a unique opportunity to direct the accelerated growth of scientific knowledge and know-how complexity amid financial pressure, an unstable industrial market, and new market expectations (Saguy 2011). Economic growth includes innovation, including technological competitiveness, which addresses performance improvement through the introduction of new market access (Bogliacino and Pianta 2011; Petrariu et al. 2013). Also, cost competitiveness focused on innovation substitutes human labor processes and industry know-how, which assumes flexibility and which cuts production costs (Bogliacino and Pianta 2011; Petrariu et al. 2013). Innovation must include developing a novel product or a meaningful improvement in existing products, thereby generating a process innovative to industries, developing new markets, developing unique sources of a supply chain, and changing the industrial landscape (Anderson et al. 2014; Azis and Osada 2010). Also, innovation must include new value creation and new network structures (Arlbjørn, de Haas, and Munksgaard 2011).

Innovation no longer results solely from the efforts of a single company; instead, companies now rely on expertise and profitable ideas from their innovation networks (Arlbjørn de Haas, and Munksgaard. 2011; Arlbjørn and Paulraj 2013; Manceau et al. 2012). Collaboration with competitors, customers, and suppliers, and across a company's boundaries, is fundamental (Baker, Grinstein, and Harmancioglu 2016; Tapscott and Williams 2006). A collaboration network encompasses formal dealings with competitors, customers, and suppliers. The primary challenge for companies is to innovate to guarantee continual growth.

Innovation involves many risks. Developing new innovative products or services requires high financial cost and may yield unsure innovation results (Baker et al. 2016; Sorescu and Spanjol 2008). Even though an innovating firm can draw resources from external networks, how external systems equally benefit from innovation results across innovating organizations is unclear (Baker et al. 2016).

Innovation can occur through new knowledge or a combination of expertise, given that companies can access expertise and combine that knowledge with existing experience to discover a unique opportunity for innovation through interaction in a network (Baker et al. 2016; Molina-Morales and Martínez-Fernández 2009). Innovation and sustained growth require an adequate supply of ideas for new services, products, and processes (Bergendahl and Magnusson 2015). Innovation is necessary for success in a competitive business environment. Organizations that regularly generate novel ideas that lead to the development of products and processes often flourish and endure (Rahman and Ramos 2013).

Firms are consistently challenged to innovate as a consequence of technological advancement and the evolution of consumer expectation. As a result of this insight, many companies seem to engage more actively in generating and developing innovation ideas (Bergendahl and Magnusson 2015; Björk, Boccardelli, and Magnusson 2010). Latent in processes, products, and services is that when companies combine these three facets, novel ideas can change existing products, processes, and services, resulting in flourishing innovation creation (Rahman and Ramos 2013). Limited studies support innovation in enterprises (Caetano and Amaral 2011).

The nature of innovation, most times, requires infrastructure or reforms management that often is beyond the control of an organization; collaborative efforts of firms enable them to act together to achieve innovation (Rahman and Ramos 2013). Companies require concerted efforts by the entire firm or individuals from other firms to work together to achieve their goals. Moreover, engaging alone in innovation processes tends to be uncertain, considering the complex business environment and the resources of SMEs, where the decision-making is often restricted to the highest levels of leadership in an organization (Rahman and Ramos 2013).

Innovation is the primary source of competition. Innovation both creates value by playing a central role in the firm's development and continues the existence of organizations (Arlbjørn and Paulraj 2013). Sustaining innovation can raise many challenges, such as resistance to change and conflict regarding new changes. Addressing these challenges becomes necessary considering competition and changes in the business environment. The firm's ability to create valuable products and services using various innovative tools determines the firm's innovation capability (Jackson, Sara, and Kahai 2014). The more a firm innovates, the more it establishes values that endure. Innovation offers unique means to address the accelerated exponential growth of scientific knowledge and know-how complexity; new market expectation; and customer needs (Saguy 2011).

Innovation exploration includes the ideation and creation phases of knowledge, which result in tacit knowledge and explicit knowledge. In this context, a firm makes tactical decisions on how to acquire knowledge externally. A firm can create understanding in the organization during the innovation-exploration stage, gain insight from outside to support innovation, or collaborate with other firms to develop knowledge jointly (Oke and Kach 2012). Technologies' push and market pull forces dictate when and how companies create innovation. Technology push takes place as research and development departments discover the new technologies the organization intends to push out to customers. The push practice is effective in reaching dormant customers' needs without customers knowing until the product or service develops and launches. Technology push prevails at some research institutions and SMEs as their focus is on their core competence (Caetano and Amaral 2011). In contrast, market pull forces occur when firms have the opportunity to improve or launch new products and services. Market pull predominates because it aims to improve existing product lines following customers' market trends (Caetano and Amaral 2011).

The importance of innovation practices for firms differs according to the organization size (Coad and Rao 2008; Petrariu et al. 2013). Innovation contributes more to the rapid growth of small and new organizations that are more active in the process of product innovation than to the growth of those that have been on the market longer (Cassia, Colombelli, and Paleari 2009; Paunov 2012). Innovation investment differs from other forms of investment because innovation has more uncertainty in the rate of outcomes and has significant initial costs that firms may not recoup quickly (Hall and Lerner 2009). Innovative ideas often reside in the knowledge of staff taking part in research projects and ideas cannot likely misplace the person who has them (Paunov 2012).

Open innovation performance. Open innovation has had full recognition since its conception. Scholars and practitioners have given much attention to the phenomenon because of its influence on organization performance (Kim, Kim, and Lee 2015). Academic communities and businesses have accepted open innovation, and the practice has increasingly grown (Enkel, Gassmann, and Chesbrough 2009). The popularity of open innovation has been reflected in various academic journals that investigate open innovation, such as *Research and Development Management* and *Technovation* (Kim et al. 2015). These efforts have encouraged many researchers (Almirall and Casadesus-Masanell 2010; Caetano and Amaral 2011; Christensen, Olesen, and Kjaer 2005; Fleming and Waguespack 2007; Kim et al. 2015; Lichtenthaler 2011) and have enhanced understanding of OIT. Gassmann, Enkel, and Chesbrough (2010) categorized these studies into nine various perspectives: institutional, structural, cultural, spatial, tool based, process based, leveraging, and user based. In contrast, Huizingh (2011) grouped these studies in different ways—open innovation process, framework, and model of open innovation—which has yielded investment in exploring OIT.

OIT has amplified existing literature by integrating inward and outward knowledge transfer (Chesbrough 2006b; Lichtenthaler 2011). Many companies use inbound and outbound innovation (van de Vrande, de Jong, et al. 2009). A company's innovation practices embrace inbound and outbound processes (Lichtenthaler 2008). The literature on open innovation presents possibilities for supporting external knowledge beyond companies' boundaries (Dittrich and Duysters 2007; Lichtenthaler 2011). The broad perspective on knowledge management processes is essential because of their potential interdependencies; for example, acquisition of external know-how could limit the possibility of a firm to commercialize its in-house knowledge (Lichtenthaler 2011; Lichtenthaler and Lichtenthaler 2009).

OIT has advanced research on decisions about knowledge management activities within and outside organizations (Lichtenthaler 2011). OIT improves how firms make decisions about sourcing or generating a specific technology internally and externally. Internally developing extensive knowledge is always challenging (Cassiman and Veugelers 2006; Lichtenthaler 2011).

OIT integrated innovation management literature and technology management research have shown that open innovation connects new product development to external technology acquisition (Lichtenthaler 2011). Modern product development literature focuses more on organizations' internal activities than their external activities (Page and Schirr 2008). In contrast, earlier works on technology management research (e.g., Afuah 2001) focused on technology management process analysis that is unrelated to firms' innovation processes (Lichtenthaler 2011).

Open innovation plays an integral role in the development of small and medium enterprises, particularly in the technological sector (Yun and Mohan 2012). SMEs rely primarily on innovation capability and assets from partnerships to execute innovation strategies (Colombo, Piva, and Rossi-Lamastra 2014). Long-term encouragement in innovation with partners yields valuable results compared to short-term incentives (Fu 2012). Further, open innovation has a viable influence on companies' expertise and inertia, in addition to business model innovation and organization inertia (H. C. Huang et al. 2013). A significant relationship exists in interfirm organizations, collaboration with intermediaries, collaboration with research institutions, and innovation performance (Zeng, Xie, and Tam 2010). An interfirm organization has the strongest significant effect on innovation performance (Zeng et al. 2010).

The level of openness can influence team characteristics and tasks, such as team size or makeup, strategic influence, market and technology uncertainty, and learning distance (Kim et al. 2015). Given that SMEs have limited resources, openness is essential to thrive (Schlagwein et al. 2017). Innovation development includes openness, and innovation commercialization involves protection (Laursen and Salter 2014). Further, concave relationships involve innovation collaborations, the breadth of a company's obvious need, and the strength of the strategies (Laursen and Salter 2014). Internal research and development, technology acquisition, and research and development partnerships relate helpfully to product and service improvements, process innovation, and patenting activity (Suh and Kim 2012).

On the downside, research and development productivity and revenues regarding the number of patents declined with openness. Open innovation adoption concerning growth in number of patents was not influenced (Caputo et al. 2016). Financial performance showed a good result with openness; however, operating income declined. Understanding how openness affects growth in the organization enables more informed decisions by managers, resulting in the efficient use of open innovation practices (Caputo et al. 2016). The limited research in SMEs' use of open innovation describes how their influence and practices differ from large organization open innovation adoption (Spithoven et al. 2013; Suh and Kim 2012). In contrast, SMEs lack the resources required for successful innovation and internal research and development activities as they are not adequately equipped (Spithoven et al. 2013; Stanislawski and Lisowski 2015). The open innovation process must be set up separately for SMEs (Spithoven et al. 2013; Stanislawski and Lisowski 2015).

Open innovation opportunities. Opportunities in open innovation are accessible to academic researchers and practitioners. Chesbrough (2006c) has documented one possibility, which is the direction of knowledge flows in light of how an organization merges various aspects of open innovation. Researchers have increasingly explored some elements of open innovation (West and Bogers 2017); nonetheless, the entire concept has not been explored fully in practice. West and Bogers (2014) affirmed the idea of inbound and outbound knowledge flows, and the former is addressed in research and practice. Even with the considerable research on inbound innovation, West and Bogers (2017) argue that knowledge about outbound open innovation remains profoundly influenced by the initial anecdotal evidence of Chesbrough (2006c). Little research has explained how a single organization can combine both inbound and outbound flows (Burcharth, Knudsen, and Søndergaard 2014). As a result, more research is needed to discern how inbound and outbound open innovations complement each other (Cassiman and Valentini 2016).

Network collaboration is another opportunity in open innovation that has grown increasingly across bilateral partnerships (Chesbrough 2006c) to different network typologies of cooperation (West and Bogers 2017). Some researchers have identified these networks as alliances, communities, consortia, ecosystems, and platforms (Adner and Kapoor 2010; Pisano and Verganti 2008; Rohrbeck et al. 2009; West 2014; West and Lakhani 2008). These networks require organizations to invest in joint creation and value capture beyond their network (West 2014). The line of reasoning also finds support in companies that support ecosystems and draw other companies to generate value as they resolve their implementation concerns (Adner and Kapoor 2010; Boudreau 2010; Rohrbeck et al. 2009). Also, limited open innovation research describes such networks beyond the computing and communications industries (West and Bogers 2017).

Users of innovation research focus mainly on individuals (Bogers, Afuah, and Bastian 2010). The microfoundations of individual action in open innovation practices are also relevant to explore. Further research is needed to address opportunism, motivations, cognitive limitations, and other activities through external individuals' aspects, cocreation, and other collaborations with organizations (West and Bogers 2017). Ample opportunities exist for research on individuals in organizations because decisions about open innovation practices are interpreted and implemented by individuals; therefore, a larger body of research is needed to understand the influence of these individuals (Alexy, Henkel, and Wallin 2013; West and Bogers 2017).

Opportunities in open innovation abound in innovation services. Open innovation highlights innovation in products to the exclusion of services (West and Bogers 2017). Because of the opportunities for value creation through differentiation, open innovation varies in services as companies face different challenges in value capture (Chesbrough 2010). Open innovation demonstrates how companies can integrate service innovation and complement product innovation (Chesbrough 2010). Although little research is conducted on this topic (West and Bogers 2017), studies by Mina et al. (2014) and Mention (2011) affirmed that open-service innovation, a scarcely explored part of research, is where the novel empirical and theoretical investigation may well provide highlights on the tactical conduct of organizations.

Internal innovation climate. Innovation relates to the economy, management, and organizational culture. Three essential stages in the innovation process are new knowledge development for innovation, knowledge acquisition for development of new products and procedures, and economic benefits from new products in the market (Trott and Hartmann 2009). These stages demonstrate the interdisciplinary nature of innovation development and commercialization of innovation. Organizational learning enables a firm to embrace creativity and innovation (K. Y. Wang et al. 2015).

Innovation involves teamwork and various deployments of knowledge of different levels. Building an innovation climate through organizational culture is one of the roles of human resources. Corporate culture relates to values, beliefs, and norms of conduct. The internal climate is how a company promotes an environment that enables innovation (Oke et al. 2013). A domestic innovation climate offers possibilities for firms to explore external knowledge to improve internal innovation (Oke et al. 2013). An innovation culture helps a firm create an environment in which it can benefit from other organizations' innovation and generate effective product innovation strategies (Azadegan 2011). An innovation climate is an essential aspect of the organization and is hard to measure. An innovative climate could easily influence innovation results (Oke et al. 2013).

The reviewed literature indicated several elements common among innovative organizations such as organizational structure, which must be available to enable innovation; strategy, which upper management or strategic managers must promote to drive innovation; and learning, which facilitates new knowledge, creative ideas, and processes that encourage interaction and collaboration internally and externally. An internal innovation climate augments innovation practices and links innovation strategy to partners in a secure network (Oke, Walumbwa, and Myers 2012). Many researchers have explored the domestic precursors of technological innovation and performance outcomes. Examples include Omri (2015) on the influence of styles of leadership; Jespersen (2012) on organizational practices; and Chong, Eerde, Rutte, and Chai (2012) and Correa, Camacho, and Mosqueda (2015) on innovation performance.

Knowledge management practices enable information flow to improve organizational performance and facilitate innovation to spawn a sustainable competitive advantage (Saini 2015). Knowledge management helps organizations address problems and improve their innovation, and therefore thrive (Mageswari, Sivasubramanian, and Dath 2015). An innovation culture offers workers the opportunity to generate new ideas, assess current designs, and augment a firm's value (Bergendahl and Magnusson 2015). Establishing an innovation culture in the organization may help encourage workers to engage in innovation. The establishment of an innovation culture entails openness to novel ideas and the ability to take risks. An innovation culture requires the willingness to experiment with new ideas, the ability to stimulate new ideas, the ability to devise new solutions to solve problems, compensating workers for risk-taking behaviors, and providing structural and infrastructural support to individuals and teams (Aaltonen et al. 2015; Uduma, Wali, and Wright 2015).

Practices that are culturally rooted promote positive actions among individuals in an organization and could lead to successful innovation (Aaltonen et al. 2015; Brunswicker and Vanhaverbeke 2011). Culture includes perceptions, assumptions, and values of individuals in the organization; culture influences decisions in the organization during the process of innovation (Brunswicker and Vanhaverbeke 2011). Also, culture promotes the development of novel ideas and channels the activities of members of a firm to spin new ideas into commercial value (Brunswicker and Vanhaverbeke 2011). Diversity is an essential factor in successful innovations (Robinson and Stubberud 2015). Despite limited resources associated with SMEs, encouraging individuals in an organization to share new ideas freely could improve innovation (Robinson and Stubberud 2015). Upper management's innovative orientation enables organizations to generate an appropriate climate to support innovation (Kraiczy, Hack, and Kellermanns 2015).

The acquisition of market knowledge characterizes an integration mechanism for outside knowledge that helps one capture, understand, and deploy the knowledge base of a firm (Zhou and Li 2012). The acquisition of market knowledge promotes the chance to obtain fundamental resources from outside sources (Zhou and Li 2012). Further, sharing knowledge and information based on the justification that mutual benefits, as well as objectives, are accepted by firms participating in the innovation yields success (Philip 2011).

Small and Medium Enterprises (SMEs)

SME firms exist worldwide and play an integral role in the global economy (Islam et al. 2011; Jain and Gandhi 2015). No industry functions effectively without the presence of SMEs, given that they provide essential resources for industry development (Khatun 2015). Some elements of SMEs' role in the global economy are developing new job opportunities, providing measures to reduce income inconsistency, and promoting the efficiency of products and services (Ilegbinosa and Jumbo 2015). SMEs motivate entrepreneurs to start new businesses that can respond easily to market changes and assist in expanding activities that economically advance the global market (Islam et al. 2011). One can compare SMEs' economic performance to the production of a nation (Islam et al. 2011). SMEs comprise over 50 percent of the GDP in developed countries and 95 percent of registered businesses (Ilegbinosa and Jumbo 2015). Worldwide, SMEs have had a remarkable influence on the international economy, including the economy of the United States, where SMEs contribute to more than 50 percent of the nonfarm private GDP and have spawned about 75 percent of new employment in the economy (Ilegbinosa and Jumbo 2015).

Research on open innovation in SMEs has seen remarkable growth. Numerous studies on open innovation related to SMEs exist in the early phase, and these studies focus mostly on secondary data: managerial or conceptual (Hossain 2015). In most cases, SMEs lack the technical and administrative skills necessary to be competitive (Rahman and Ramos 2013). They become less engaged in open innovation compared to more critical organizations because of limited resources, uniqueness, and strategies (Hossain 2015). SMEs focus primarily on the selection of policies and practices (Theyel 2013). SMEs search for strategies on activities for the potential market, new knowledge, partners, and innovative ideas (Hossain 2015). SMEs can significantly develop using external resources, in some measure, by revealing internal construction to the external environment (Henkel 2006; Hossain 2015). Regional and nationwide proximities, in conjunction with external challenges to innovation, may be the primary reason SMEs seek open innovation (Othman Idrissia, Amaraa, and Landrya 2012).

SME collaboration depends on the type of activities the SME intends to engage in. Horizontal collaboration is valuable for incremental innovation, but vertical partnerships fit when considering a radical innovation (Parida, Westerberg, and Frishammar 2012). SME involvement with outside entities boosts their chance to implement novel ideas, products, and services (Spithoven et al. 2013). SMEs use open innovation to join forces on new product development and closed innovation to pool resources on incremental improvement to available products (Wynarczyk 2013). The collaboration of SMEs becomes more decisive during the commercialization phase of innovation than earlier on (Hemert, Nijkamp, and Masurel 2013; Hossain 2015; van de Vrande et al. 2009). SME collaboration is beyond science and know-how; it also comprises value chain partnerships' offering knowledge bases that are easily absorbed (Spithoven et al. 2013).

Networking is another useful way SMEs can involve outside innovation. SMEs can benefit from network practices employed to foresee possibilities (Heger 2014; Heger and Boman 2015). An SME's innovation mainly relies on networks with other SME organizations (Hemert et al. 2013). Knowledge-based open innovation is the driver of social network constructs that encourage horizontal collaboration networks (McAdam et al. 2014).

Implementing consistent network practices can lead to higher innovation performance (Pullen et a. 2012). In contrast, using multiple interfaces can be challenging for SMEs. SMEs may trade off between extensive and intensive networks, but they are cautious concerning the network's parties (Hughes 2009). In most cases, SMEs network more efficiently with customers than with suppliers.

Open Innovation in SMEs

Colombo et al. (2014) asserted that open innovation research in SMEs is disjointed. Earlier work on open innovation focused mainly on open innovation adaptation practices and approaches in large organizations like IBM and Procter & Gamble (Chesbrough 2006c). Even though limited, the growing research on SMEs has shown that open innovation is not solely for more prominent organizations but is for SME adaptation and practices as well (Wynarczyk 2013). Following the guidance of Parida et al. (2012), SMEs could gain more from open innovation than bigger companies because they respond quickly to changes in the market and are more willing to take risks. The acceptance of open innovation practices benefits SMEs that use the technologies and knowledge that is developed by other organizations and shared through collaboration networks to advance innovation (Crema et al. 2014; Whittaker, Fath, and Fiedler 2016). The adoption of open innovation is necessary for SMEs' growth and competition in the marketplace (Csath 2012). SMEs should have a learning system that promotes creativity, collaboration, and openness; accepts criticism; is self-motivated; and includes continuous learning (Csath 2012).

SMEs face numerous challenges in innovation implementation. Most SMEs face difficulties in stimulating innovation because they lack the resources and competencies required for such investments (Talegeta 2014). These challenges include operational coordination functions (Abouzeedan, Klofsten, and Hedner 2013), external networking, external participation, customer involvement, venturing, and research and development (van de Vrande et al. 2009).

Open innovation presents viable opportunities for SMEs. Oakey (2013) criticized Chesbrough for overemphasizing the scope to which companies can implement open innovation, given that research and development are often expensive, risky, and long term, and necessitate considerable protection of outcomes. Oakey argued that a more effective path for research and development projects is closed innovation. Xiaobao, Wei, and Yuzhen (2013) believed that SMEs that embrace open innovation would improve in their business operations and better compete. Török and Tóth (2013) posited that mutual exchange boosts the chances of SMEs to realize substantial benefits for their involvement with other firms in developing a new product.

Construction Industry

The construction industry plays a fundamental part in the social and economic growth of a nation and often reflects on the nation's contribution to the GDP (Perez, González-Cruz, and Pastor-Ferrando 2010; Sev 2009). Construction investments include technological operations and usually require rearrangement in multiple parts when examining technical precedence (Vanhoucke 2011). Many construction projects are delayed and generate lower efficiencies, often interpreted as budget overruns and an unnecessary waste of materials and natural resources (Perez et al. 2010). Managing a construction project involves several participants; examples include construction firms, end users, project developers, promoters, suppliers, subcontractors, and governments (Perez et al. 2010). The end product of construction projects is usually complex and unique because each project uses specific technology and human resources. Building and engineering projects have a detailed construction plan, design specifications, and technical specifications (Perez et al. 2010).

Leadership is fundamental in the construction industry and a significant factor in upholding sustainable practices in the construction sector (Opoku, Ahmed, and Cruickshank 2015). Construction firms need management that offers collective vision, strategy, and direction toward achieving organizational goals (Opoku et al. 2015). Researchers have paid attention to how those in a leadership role improve innovation performance in the construction industry (Bossink 2007; Opoku et al. 2015).

Many factors affect construction industry competitiveness. Examples include the integrated performance of supporting industries, the workforce, and government support (Deng, Liu, and Jin 2013). Providing quality services and ensuring customers are satisfied are ways firms can differentiate themselves from competitors (Duljevic and Poturak 2017). Customer satisfaction plays an integral part in the development and management of the construction process and the development of professional–customer relationships. Customer satisfaction is a critical determinant of project completion and one fundamental concern of construction managers who frequently explore means to improve performance to endure in the marketplace (Duljevic and Poturak 2017).

Some researchers discussed the value of organizational learning in the construction industry (Koskinen 2012; Santos-Vijande, López-Sánchez, and Trespalacios 2012). Organizational learning has become a fundamental and sustainable means to increase construction industry growth (Pheng, Shang, and Foong 2016). Learning in the construction industry can emerge from internal activities and by way of planning, organizing, and implementing projects (Tennant and Fernie 2013). The learning process starts with individuals learning from others (Pheng et al. 2016). By sharing knowledge and skills, organization members learn from inside the organization. Learning is relatively dynamic and active in the construction sectors (Pheng et al. 2016).

Furthermore, the construction industry is often perceived as a sector that affects the environment destructively because of the excessive consumption of resources (al-Maian et al. 2015; Ding 2008). Some environmental issues connected to construction practices include desertification, ozone depletion, climate change, and acidification (al-Maian et al. 2015). Society increasingly draws attention to factors beyond the economic growth of the construction sectors, such as the long-term effect that construction has on present and future generations (Waas, Verbruggen, and Wright 2010).

The construction industry has several challenges, including the fragmented nature of the sector, which results in ineffective coordination and poor communication (Pheng et al. 2016). The uniqueness of every project, which poses problems in capturing the desirable parts of each project and in the reuse of practices for upcoming projects, and the fact that plans are often complex and extensive makes documentation complicated to manage. Also, the construction industry faces challenges related to the supply chain. The supply chain supporting construction projects is extensive and profound, resulting in difficulties in managing the various networks of independent contractors, subcontractors, and suppliers (al-Maian et al. 2015). Because of the multiple entities involved, continuing efforts must ensure construction project equipment, materials, and products meet required specifications and are delivered to the project site without the need for rework (al-Maian et al. 2015). The poor performance of construction projects because of delays, cost overruns, disputes, adversarial relationships, customer dissatisfaction, and low productivity stems from a variety of approaches including risk transfer, fragmentation, and inadequate collaboration (G. Chen et al. 2012).

Additionally, construction workers face challenges and casualties at work. The construction sector has elevated fatality rates compared to other sectors (E. W. Cheng et al. 2015). The project may have unsafe construction sites and expose workers to high-risk jobs (E. W. Cheng et al. 2015). Researchers have identified some factors that could improve the safety of construction workers, such as an incentive distribution method, appropriate labor training, specialized work, and safety and security equipment (E. W. Cheng et al. 2015; Hasan and Jha 2013).

Middle managers in the construction industry. Middle managers are central to organization innovation (H. Cheng, Song, and Li 2017). They search for and implement innovation (Bourne and Walker 2005; Chinyamurindi 2016). A middle manager is an individual at the management level below individuals in upper management who implement a firm's broad responsibilities (Chinyamurindi 2016; Herzig and Jimmieson 2006). Middle managers execute five essential tasks: setting objectives, distributing resources, participating in management, communicating, and managing human resources (Johansen and Hawes 2016). The primary role of middle managers is to execute those decisions planned by upper management. In achieving this, middle managers remain guided by experience and the ability to become strategic and operational (Salih and Doll 2013).

Creating awareness of the importance of middle managers' commitment to new ideas and initiatives can influence employees' commitment to innovative initiatives (Alhaqbani et al. 2016). When a firm lacks the determination of its middle managers, it experiences difficulty in implementing new ideas, which can cause a setback in the implementation process. The commitment of middle managers is essential to ensuring valuable ideas are implemented successfully at lower units of the organization (Alhaqbani et al. 2016). Developing and training middle managers improves their knowledge base, expectations, and personal targets (Abugre and Adebola 2015) and helps establish managerial provisions of feedback (Van den Bossche, Segers, and Jansen 2010).

Management practices in the construction industry. The advancement in know-how and the changes experienced in various scientific fields have shaped project management and have caused its environmental conditions to become even more complicated than in the past (Makui, Moeinzadeh, and Bagherpour 2017). Most recently, because of advances in know-how used in project implementation, the scale of projects and the scope have developed to acquire an expanded supply chain and project stakeholders (Makui et al. 2017). A delay is a practical problem that construction management tends to address and is the most often recurring setback in the industry (al-Sehaimi et al. 2014). Studies in this field focus on descriptive and explanatory research, making it problematic to concentrate on pressing managerial problems (al-Sehaimi et al. 2014). Factors associated with poor project management concern mostly delays in the field, even though it differs in importance from the results of various studies (Koskela, Tzortzopoulos, and al-Sehaimi 2013). Such delays tend to cluster around the management and project environment (Koskela et al. 2013).

Management factors include poor site management, inadequate planning and control, poor communication between the entities involved, and unstable accessibility of resources. These factors may not be under control, and efforts should be directed at reducing their consequence (Koskela et al. 2013). In contrast, project environment factors include problems related to material supply, labor shortage, and finances. These factors link to the immaturity of the economy, the business organization, and the labor market and are external factors that must be considered in each particular project (al-Sehaimi et al. 2014; Koskela et al. 2013).

Management practices are viable when appropriately channeled to benefit the organization. The culture of an organization shapes its management practices (Chan and Tse 2003; P. Chen, Partington, and Qiang 2009). Culture determines a variety of management practices (Chan and Tse 2003).

Ofori-Boadu et al. (2012) supported implementing management practices under the Malcolm Baldrige National Quality Award criteria:

- Leadership involves leading and motivating individuals to attain the goals and objects of their organization (Ofori-Boadu et al. 2012). Leaders should be fully committed to encouraging members to be committed to their organization.
- Strategic planning highlights the operational plans of an organization to guarantee business results. Companies must design strategic plans to be flexible and to endure political and economic variations (Kazaz and Ulubeyli 2009). Strategic planning can help an organization outperform others that are not implementing strategic plans (al-Shammari and Hussein 2007).
- Customer focus outlines customer satisfaction and competition. These involve measuring, analyzing, and managing knowledge to address information management, implementation, and performance.
- Workforce focus addresses issues related to human resources, such as recruitment, selection, placement, employee motivation, and training.
- Operations focus involves implementing effective operations and procedures.

Synthesis of the Research Findings

The primary focus of the literature review was a review of OIT as the framework for the study and a discussion of the topic of management practices and innovation, SMEs, and the construction industry. OIT allows the innovation process to take place through collaboration with other organizations, entities, individuals, customers, suppliers, research laboratories, universities, and so forth (Chesbrough 2006b) to facilitate a smooth flow of ideas beyond organizational boundaries. The goal of open innovation is to drive benefits from the exploration of internal and external resources (Chesbrough 2006c).

One fundamental notion found in the review of literature is that most studies on open innovation have queried large organizations, such as Procter & Gamble and IBM, with vast evidence indicating the need for more studies on the various perspectives not only of sizable high-technology organizations but also of low-technology firms, particularly SMEs. Interest in this area derived from the assumption that OIT facilitates knowledge about the use of management practices to define innovation processes in SMEs in the construction industry. In this context, researchers concluded that open innovation may not only add to the body of research on management practices and innovation but also could prompt the interest of academic researchers and practitioners to consider issues that influence innovation in SMEs in the construction industry. In further exploration of OIT, a gap in the literature emerged in addressing the relationship between management practices and innovation.

Because of limited research on how OIT relates to the use of management practices that contribute to innovation in SMEs in the construction industry, little attention has accrued to SMEs' innovation processes in mainstream research (Wynarczyk 2013). OIT is the backbone of public sources. Openness in innovation practices stems from shorter innovation cycles and industrial research (Eservel 2014). Openness is a source of external knowledge that an organization acquires through innovation activities (Conboy and Morgan 2011). Open innovation includes various internal and external sources for improving innovation (Conboy and Morgan 2011). The available literature implies that open sources influence how SMEs conduct research and development (Trott and Hartmann 2009) and, therefore, can leverage open innovation to boost resources and capabilities and improve innovation performance.

In open innovation literature, the emphasis was on external interactions. Interaction points to the extent to which open innovation relates to other forms of innovation. Through interactions, companies enhance their opportunities and exchange novel ideas (Trott and Hartmann 2009). Firms with the capacity to conduct in-house research and development are in better shape to access external information (Trott and Hartmann 2009). Research and development departments can identify the value of interactions beyond organizations' boundaries. Firms can make a considerable effort to develop SMEs' capacity to interact internally and externally. The idea is to see that open innovation facilitates the development of know-how across business boundaries.

Open innovation should be viewed in different forms. Researchers such as Chesbrough (2017) and West and Bogers (2017) describe open innovation as practices centered on knowledge flow that involve accessing, harnessing, and absorbing the flow of knowledge beyond companies' boundaries. In outside-in open innovation, a firm opens its innovation process to external knowledge inputs (Chesbrough 2006c, 2012, 2017). Also, inside-out open innovation denotes the ability of a firm to allow other firms to access their unused and underused resources and knowledge (Chesbrough 2006c, 2012, 2017; Hossain 2013).

Companies can achieve positive results when they develop the ability to learn (Tzortzaki and Mihiotis 2014). Such knowledge can improve when firms intentionally use new practices that encourage members to create and to share their capabilities to perform. Researchers identified two strategies to manage knowledge: personalization strategy, based on developed networks that facilitate tacit knowledge sharing, and codification strategy, which relates to the electronic structure used to store and disseminate information to foster knowledge recycling (Tzortzaki and Mihiotis 2014). Further, codification strategy can be used to guide managerial decisions on practices that can protect knowledge acquired internally from rivals or imitators, whereas the personalization strategy shows details about adopted networks in the process of sharing tacit knowledge in the organization (Tzortzaki and Mihiotis 2014).

The review of the literature on open innovation presents several concepts. Various academic researchers and practitioners have explored these concepts. For example, researchers Saleim and Khalil (2011) studied the relationship between knowledge management and intellectual capital. Salavati and Madah (2008) and Saleim and Khalil (2011) indicated that knowledge-based corporate enterprises derive advantages from the outcome of innovations and new ideas coming from the interaction between human capital and organization structure. Ren, Wang, Yang, and Wei (2013) investigated internal and external network competence related to a company's innovation outcomes. Akhavan and Pezeshkan (2014) and Saleim and Khalil (2011) found that companies must manage information efficiently between individuals and firms to develop innovations.

Researchers such as Buganza, Chiaroni, Colombo, and Frattini (2011), Enkel, Gassmann, and Chesbrough (2009), Keupp and Gassmann (2009), and Lazzarotti, Manzini, and Pellegrini (2010) explored open innovation regarding diversification of partnerships. Van de Vrande, Lemmens, and Vanhaverbeke (2006) investigated open innovation concerning acquisition. In this context, the researchers considered open innovation to be about network partnerships, including customers and employees.

The literature implies that managers stimulate innovation through collaborative networks and creativity in the sense that managers generate new ideas that lead to know-how development with external partners, know-how that they would not otherwise have been able to achieve without such interactions. Capozzi, Dye, and Howe (2011) suggested that a collaborative system can develop into a creative team and spark innovation. Ren et al. (2013) corroborated that external networks are useful resources to facilitate innovations. Birkinshaw and Robbins (2010) and Rampersad, Quester, and Troshani (2010) found that external networks aid access to novel ideas and boost the innovation capacity of organizations.

Studies reviewed concerning OIT revealed that despite the strengths of open innovation, limitations and challenges exist (Chesbrough 2017). OIT advocates open interaction and supports learning and knowledge sharing. Sharing information with external entities to succeed in acquiring new skills can result in the leakage of key, sensitive knowledge, posing a real risk (Huston and Sakkab 2007; Trott and Hartmann 2009). Organizations involved in research and development alliances face the challenge of sustaining the proper open knowledge exchange required for such collaborative research development goals while managing information flows to reduce the risk of unintentional leakage of sensitive knowledge (Trott and Hartmann 2009). Researchers have given thought to the problem of loss of knowledge and information in the innovation management literature (Trott and Hartmann 2009). Companies that participate in collaborative innovation need to be open to knowledge sharing with partners to benefit from the collaborative efforts.

Critique of Previous Research Methods

Regardless of the growing interest in open innovation, research related to its application in SMEs is scarce in a mainstream publication (Lee et al. 2010). This section presents a critique of some previous research concerning open innovation in the construction industry SMEs relevant to the study. Rahman and Ramos (2013) explored the challenges of adopting strategies for SME open innovation. The researchers focused on the implementation of open innovation practices in SMEs aligned with financial, technological, managerial, and policy issues. In their study, Rahman and Ramos used a questionnaire on the Survey Monkey site to collect data from fifty-one organizations in the SME sector selected to participate in a Web-based survey. The findings revealed an abundance of studies, practices, and case studies on open innovation practices in the larger organization, but few of these were about SMEs. The researchers discovered that high wage levels generate a scarcity of a skilled workforce, leading to a shortage of skilled resources and the purchase of a workforce because of scarce economic resources. Also, the high cost of innovation and of knowledge about open innovation strategies played an essential part in the adoption of open innovation in SMEs.

Ofori-Boadu et al. (2012), in a qualitative research study, addressed management practices in the context of Leadership in Energy and Environment Design (LEED). Ofori-Boadu et al. focused a survey of six US contractors selected from the top one hundred green contractors involved in LEED project management practices implementation. As in several other qualitative types of research, the researchers used structured case study interviews as a data collection approach. Their findings supported implementing management practices categorized by Malcolm Baldrige National Quality Award criteria, which are fundamental to the implementation of LEED designs. The sample in the Ofori-Boadu et al. study was relatively small compared to sample sizes used by most qualitative researchers in similar research. Despite the small sample size used, the size was appropriate for the limited number of participating organizations.

P. Chen, Partington, and Qiang (2009) used a case study to analyze the influence of climate on regular construction work activities. The researchers focused on factors that caused construction project delay and also studied the scope by which weather variables obstructed outside construction work. The researchers processed the climatic data using simple calculations to generate a series of quantitative maps and tables valuable for construction planners to determine the appropriate time to initiate a project and the location to build projects. Their analysis focused on a real case of the construction of various bridges in southern Chile. The researchers noted that the simplified approach used was entirely transferable to other countries, except the combination of weather variables might differ by country. P. Chen, Partington, and Qiang concluded that the weather influence on projects was referenced as the source of construction delay, but studies addressing this topic are rare.

Various studies reviewed pointed to the need to balance management practices with sustainable growth. A good example is a study conducted by al-Sehaimi et al. (2014) on the most recent planning system to improve construction management practices. The researchers collected data using questionnaires, observation, and interviews. They executed the previous planner system using an action research process in two state-owned construction projects. The findings showed that several factors hindered the realization of the last planner system, such as attitude to time and subcontractors' and individuals' commitment. Better communication, improved construction planning, site management improvement, and coordination between entities were identified as advantages of the previous planner system. Al-Sehaimi et al. concluded that these improvements were possible through knowledge expansion and learning, quality of work practice, and enhancement of managerial practices.

After a careful analysis of recent literature regarding open innovation, the conclusion was that most studies on open innovation centered more on quantitative analysis, ignoring exploration of more profound meanings of the identified modes (Rangus 2017), which is indicative of a gap in the study of open innovation. Huizingh (2011) confirmed that open innovation had gained substantial attention among academics and practitioners. The increasing interest yet lack of research on open innovation could draw attention to more research methods to complement existing studies by linking quantitative and qualitative methods (Rangus 2017). The research gap points to the need for more reviews in the qualitative methodology, and to longitudinal studies as well as mixed-method studies. Firms now search for innovative practices to enhance their business activities and competition through open innovation and harnessing external ideas to leverage research and develop across company operations (Chesbrough 2006c).

The methodology selected for the study was an exploratory qualitative inquiry, because of its helpfulness in adding knowledge to the topic of investigation. By using an exploratory qualitative method to explore the perceptions of middle managers in SMEs in the construction industry, insight was gained regarding the relationship between management practices and innovation. OIT informed the study because it elucidates how managers use management practices to facilitate business operations and achieve better results. Openness draws various pools of expertise and necessary resources externally to complement inside innovation (Almirall and Casadesus-Masanell 2010).

Although the review of the literature showed increasing interest in open innovation among scholars and practitioners, some studies focused on larger companies. The information discovered in the research is congruent with the practices of OIT, which emphasizes the importance of firms' opening their innovation processes to other firms. Open innovation activities can help SMEs prevail over challenges of limited resources and engage in more open innovation practices to improve business outcomes (Gassmann et al. 2010).

Summary

The review of the literature has revealed important facets of open innovation in the construction sector SMEs. Management practices and innovation research are limited in top journals concerning SMEs in the construction industry. Studies about open innovation in SMEs appeared widely in journals. Open innovation in SMEs appeared more productive in commercialization than in the early phase of development.

Compared to large organizations, SMEs should be cautious about protecting intellectual property before collaborating with partners. Carefully reviewing and safeguarding intellectual property before working with others is prudent. Research related to open innovation in SMEs primarily addresses the technology of SMEs. More research is needed to determine the role of management practices in US SMEs in the construction industry. The current study was intended to convey more clarity on this question.

METHODOLOGY

Chapter 3 imparts a discussion of the methods used in the current study. The relationship between management practices and innovation in SMEs in the construction industry of the United States was investigated using an exploratory qualitative method. Semistructured interviews were conducted with middle managers in construction industry SMEs. The chapter presents details about the methodology used for the exploratory qualitative study. The chapter includes the purpose of the study, the research question, the research design, the target population and sample, procedures, instruments, and ethical considerations. The procedures section provides details about participant selection, protection of participants, data collection, and data analysis, as well as an overview of the expert review before presenting the study. Also, the instrument section includes details concerning the role of the researcher and the guiding interview questions.

Purpose of the Study

The purpose of the exploratory qualitative study was to investigate the constructs of OIT to determine how middle manager practices may facilitate innovations in construction industry SMEs. The central constructs of OIT consist of collaborative innovation and innovation networks. The qualitative method and an exploratory design were used to explore the perceptions of middle managers who have worked three or more years in an SME in the construction industry. The primary topic of the study was management practices and innovation related to middle managers in SMEs in the construction industry. In the study, the relationship between management practices and innovation in SMEs was explored because SMEs are significant to economic growth (Karadag 2015). Exploring this relationship was meant to align OIT with the construction industry SMEs. Knowledge of how various management practices may lead to innovation development can help facilitate the growth of SMEs.

The economic relevance of SMEs is fundamental. Regardless of the growing interest in OIT research, studies on OIT in SMEs have been scarce in mainstream research (Wynarczyk 2013), likely because researching smaller firms is often more challenging than researching larger firms. Because of limited resources for innovation, the need to develop superior products and to share risks allied to establishing innovation lead SMEs to collaborate with partners and networks to innovate (Wagner 2012). Collaboration with companies that aim to innovate could facilitate the sharing of knowledge, information, and experiences, thereby improving how companies learn and work (Malmström et al. 2013).

Research Question

In conducting exploratory qualitative research, asking research questions that provide insight into the phenomena under investigation is required. Inquiries into relevant questions are a critical part of conducting research (Tenenberg 2014). The research question should be central to guide the method of research (Hansen and Trifković 2015). The research question to investigate the phenomena of construction industry management practices and innovation was: What roles do management practices have in innovation in US SMEs in the construction industry?

Research Design

The exploratory qualitative study design was used to gain more knowledge about the phenomena under investigation. An exploratory qualitative approach is valuable because the method allows for an exploration of the attitudes and experiences of the individuals under investigation (Percy et al. 2015). Also, qualitative research allows researchers to comprehend and elucidate the conduct of people and evaluate the world around them (Gergen, Josselson, and Freeman 2015). In this case, an exploratory qualitative inquiry was useful in discovering the perceptions of middle managers to determine how they contribute to innovation through management practices in the construction industry SMEs.

The research question investigated, through an exploratory qualitative methodology, how middle managers in the construction industry SMEs contribute to innovation through management practices. Exploratory qualitative inquiry is a way to examine people's experiences as they reflect on the external world (Percy et al. 2015). The exploratory qualitative research inquiry is a useful approach to investigate the personal beliefs and experiences of individuals in a way that other qualitative research methods do not do. Exploratory qualitative research methodology centers on the external or real world to assist in understanding how individuals apportion meaning to social reality or human reality and uses people's words to explain the phenomena under study (Collins and Cooper 2014; Hickson 2011). Also, Allwood's (2012) guidance was followed concerning gathering participant perceptions from their points of view and lived experiences.

The qualitative methodology permits a researcher to obtain data based on the experiences of study participants. Following Percy et al. (2015), the qualitative inquiry explored subjective opinions. Qualitative inquiry addresses ambiguous phenomena and presents significant corroboration from lived experience (Birchall 2014). Locke's (2011) direction was followed regarding using qualitative research inquiry to employ inductive reasoning and flexible approaches where conclusions about data and analysis developed as the research progressed. Inductive reasoning has, at its core, a focus on the researcher to investigate and construct meaning from the data as findings emerge (Soltanifar and Ansari 2016). The research methodology was used to discover the complex experiences of middle managers in the construction industry SMEs' innovation practices.

In the study, an exploratory qualitative design incorporated concepts to understand the perception of middle managers and innovation. Exploratory qualitative research exhibits the characteristics of a qualitative research methodology but does not require a specific method or framework (Sandelowski 2000). Figure 1 shows the research design. The research design represents underpinning study concepts. The figure demonstrates the interrelated domains investigated regarding OIT, management practices, and innovation. The research design was used to explore the experiences of middle managers to achieve a conclusive result about the topic under investigation.

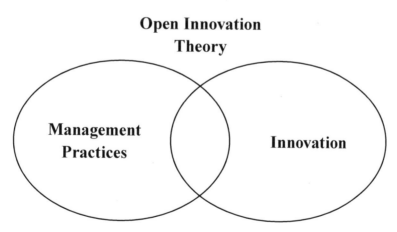

Figure 1. Research design diagram.

Target Population and Sample

In selecting the target population for the study, a purposive sampling technique was used to include participants with common characteristics, specifically, middle managers employed in SMEs in the construction industry. Researchers can select target populations that include individuals from the same group who exhibit a variety of experiences and provide adequate data regarding the topic under investigation (Malterud, Siersma, and Guassora 2016). Participants with characteristics that were relative to the phenomena under study were specifically targeted.

To obtain the quality of data required in qualitative research, Eide and Kahn (2008) suggested "a mutual standpoint, researcher to the participant, human being to human being" (199). When adequate interaction takes place between the participants and the researcher, a smaller number of participants provide the necessary information to explore the phenomena under investigation (Malterud et al. 2016). A variety of factors, such as the researcher's or participant's skills or ability to articulate, determines the quality of interaction through information imparted. Even though the sample size in qualitative research tends to be small (Mason 2010), a suitable sample size was necessary to guarantee that the study results were reliable.

Population

The population for the qualitative exploratory study included middle managers in SMEs in the construction industry. These managers provided a variety of experiences about innovation, collaboration, problem solving, planning, implementing decision-making processes, directing people, and overseeing capabilities and the resources of their organizations (Bager et al. 2015; Szczepańska-Woszczyna 2014), all of which were important for the topic under study. Limited industry scope provided the chance for a range of middle managers in construction industry SMEs who were involved in various management practices and innovation. It is also noted that the construction industry is male-dominated (Wright 2014).

Sample

A sample size of twenty was targeted for the exploratory qualitative inquiry. Even though no specific rules exist about sample size in qualitative studies, a sample size of twenty was appropriate for the study as similar sample sizes exist in qualitative research (Bellucci 2016). Determining sample size in qualitative research "is contextual and partially dependent upon the scientific paradigm under which investigation is taking place" (Boddy 2016, 426). The sample size in the study yielded sufficient feedback on the phenomena under inquiry. A sample size between five and fifty respondents is an appropriate number for qualitative studies (Dworkin 2012; Mason 2010). Researchers established that in qualitative research, the general concept for sample size is saturation

(Boddy 2016; Guest, Bunce, and Johnson 2006). In conducting a qualitative study, an adequate sample is fundamental to completing credible research because researchers can obtain enough data that is an antecedent to careful analysis and findings (Marshall et al. 2013).

The inclusion criteria comprised employees in middle management positions with three or more years of experience in an SME within the construction industry who were involved in innovation. Middle managers who did not meet the inclusion criteria were excluded. The managers have expertise and experience in innovation. These managers provided various experiences about innovation, collaboration, problem solving, planning, implementing the decision-making process, directing people, and overseeing capabilities and the resources of their organization, all of which enriched the study.

Sample Frame

The sample frame for the exploratory qualitative research was Qualtrics's panel of eligible participants and subsequent snowball sampling. Twenty interviewees were initially targeted. On the topic of recruiting study participants from third parties, Arend (2014) recommended that researchers consider the quality of their recruitment and the validity of the entire process. Although Qualtrics provided an accurate representation of the US population, based on data of individuals who indicated their interest to participate in the study, additional participants were sourced using snowball recruiting to achieve saturation.

Procedures

In conducting academic research, study guidelines are necessary to uphold the integrity of a study. This section presents the guidelines approved for the research to facilitate the completion of the predetermined goals. The procedures included are participant selection, protection of participants, expert review, data collection, and data analysis. Observing these guidelines was critical to study completion.

In the exploratory qualitative research, the following procedures were followed:

1. *Participant selection.* Participant selection was of middle managers who had three or more years of working experience in SMEs in the construction industry.
2. *Participant protection.* Participants' identifiable information was secured through alphanumeric codes.

3. *Data collection.* A semistructured interview and guided questions were used to obtain data from participants.

4. *Data analysis.* The process of data analysis was through NVivo 12 Pro.

Participant Selection

In conducting exploratory qualitative research, participant selection is viable only when researchers select those who can provide the best information. Cleary, Horsfall, and Hayter (2014) recommended choosing participants broadly because of their experience or knowledge of the phenomena under investigation. Following Sargeant's (2012) guidelines, participants were selected based on the research question, inclusion criteria, theoretical perspective, and data informing the research. During this process, numerous steps were taken to ensure that the participant selection process was inclusive.

The initial step of finding participants was to obtain a license from Qualtrics, which involved securing site permission and using the Qualtrics network to recruit participants. The inclusion criteria were sent to Qualtrics by email. Qualtrics began to identify and procure eligible participants from their network. The contact information of participants was made available on the recruitment Web page. With the contact information, the participants were contacted through email to schedule interviews.

The participant recruitment process was more complicated than expected. Qualtrics recruited for several months, identifying fifty-nine potential participants, but only five completed the interview process. At that point, Qualtrics discontinued participant recruitment. Because Qualtrics failed to comply with the agreement to provide enough participants, they provided a refund for the originally contracted services.

Snowball recruiting was employed to recruit additional respondents, by contacting them via email or text messages. Snowball recruiting was conducted by asking the five participants if they knew of anyone else who met the study criteria. The five participants, after receiving permission from the potential participants to forward their information, provided the names and contact information of an additional twenty-five potential participants. The twenty-five additional participants were contacted through email and text messages. The informed consent form was emailed after participants indicated their interest to participate in the study. Twenty participants signed the informed consent forms via email within two business days. The other five participants never responded. Among the twenty who accepted to participate in the study, only seven eventually completed an interview.

Participant Protection

In conducting qualitative research, the researcher must consider participants' welfare before initiating contact with the potential participants. Ross, Iguchi, and Panicker (2018) advised ensuring "participants are fully informed and comprehend the risks of harm inherent in participating in the study" (141). In the study, the informed consent form was used to ensure that participants were fully aware of their rights in the study. The informed consent form outlined the study objectives, including the procedures, confidentiality of information, the privacy of participants, and foreseeable risks or benefits of participation in the study. The informed consent form specified the security measures used to safeguard information provided by participants.

A unique identifier to protect the study participants' identities was provided for each participant (for example, "001"). Any identifying information of participants was removed from the data collected from interviews. The coded documentation did not include identifiable information. Security codes and passwords were assigned to computerized data, and each participant was assigned a separate folder and code where documents about his or her participation were reserved, such as consent forms, interview notes, and interview transcripts.

The master code sheet was stored separately from the data in a combination safe. Interview records and transcripts were saved in a document on an external hard drive, locked and secured with a password, and paper documents related to the study were kept in a secured file cabinet. After seven years, related study documents will be shredded and burned, such as paper copies of study information, and electronic media that contains information and participant data will be reformatted and erased.

At the beginning of each telephonic interview, voluntary participation was emphasized, and the participant was told that the interview would be recorded. Participants were informed that their responses to the interview questions and their personal information were confidential and protected. Participants were informed they could stop the interview at will or when they wished to ask for clarification on any question they did not understand. Each interview initiated once the participants provided consent for the interview to begin. The interview protocol was used to conduct this telephonic interview. Rapport was developed with each participant, which assisted in readily finding common ground with participants, thereby facilitating mutual understanding and enabling interactions to flow well in the interviews. The flow of communication made most of the interviews productive (Alsaawi 2014; Mann 2011). At the end of each interview, participants were informed that the interview transcript would be sent to them for review and verification of accuracy. Participants were asked to make corrections to their interview responses and return them via email with changes. Member checking aligns with Alsaawi's (2014) and Mann's (2011) recommendations.

Expert review. A request was sent through email to six potential expert members. The email provided detailed information about the study and the reason for the expert review of the study. Three individuals agreed to participate and provide feedback. The other three individuals who were approached did not agree to participate in the expert review.

The expert panel included a senior qualitative researcher and School of Business and Technology dissertation lead, an executive professional consultant, and an associate professor in a school of business and global innovation, all with the knowledge and skills to provide feedback and recommendations on the qualitative interview questions. Panel members were selected because of their expertise in qualitative research and innovation. The expert panel members each had a doctorate and understood the dissertation process. The primary goal of the expert panel was to review the proposed interview questions aligned with the research question and provide feedback. The expert panel provided input and recommendations that enhanced the study interview questions. The expert review ended within four weeks.

Mock interviews. Mock interviews were conducted with two colleagues who matched the study inclusion criteria. Each mock interview lasted thirty to forty minutes. According to Powell, Hughes-Scholes, Cavezza, and Stoové (2010), researchers should use mock interviews "for the purposes of interviewer assessment and training" (244). Mock interviews provided practice for the interview process.

Data Collection

In conducting data analysis, a researcher can use several methods: conducting interviews, employing a focus group, and observing. An interview is the commonly used data collection method in qualitative research (Peters and Halcomb 2015); researchers mainly use structured, semistructured, or unstructured interviews. Semistructured interviews are flexible because they incorporate specific questions about the topic under study and allow a researcher to follow responses from participants thoroughly (Kallie et al. 2016). In conducting the research, audio-recorded semistructured interviews were used to gather data. A semistructured interview permits a researcher to collect detailed information in as brief a time as fifteen minutes or in several hours (Cachia and Millward 2011). The interview process depends on the researcher and the type of phenomena under investigation.

Prequalification screening. During the screening process, potential participants each identified if they worked as a middle manager in an SME in the construction industry, had been involved in innovation, and had three or more years of working experience in one or more SMEs in the construction industry. Once eligibility was determined, those participants automatically were directed to the informed consent form on the Qualtrics website. After the study participants identified had acknowledged the informed consent form, they were emailed a Doodle scheduling tool to allow them to select the time and date they would prefer for the telephonic interview. When participants picked a specific time frame, that time became blocked so other participants could not book the same time slot. The participants who had been recruited via snowballing also used the Doodle scheduling tool. The informed consent form was sent to those participants by email, which they signed and returned by email within two business days. Three days before each interview, a notification was sent to participants through email with a calendar reminder.

Interviews. Before beginning interviews, a notation was made of the date and time of the conversation, and an identifier unique to each participant was assigned, such as 001. Participants were told the purpose of the inquiry, the research question, and their role in the study. They were also notified of their rights to participate in or leave the study at will without opposition. The average interview time was thirty-five minutes five seconds. The lengthiest interview lasted forty-five minutes. The shortest time was twenty-five minutes. I was in a secured private room to avoid any interruptions during interviews. After the participants responded to the questions, they were asked if they had any questions, then I thanked them for their time. After each interview, bracketing, a process based on self-reflection, where the researcher works to suppress biases and knowledge of the phenomena under study, was used (Tufford and Newman 2010). In this work bracketing helped ensure that personal bias did not influence the study's integrity.

Audio files and interview transcripts. After the interviews, I transcribed the recorded audio within seven days. The transcripts were emailed to participants, who then were asked to provide feedback within ten business days. Each participant was asked if he or she would like to arrange a follow-up interview. Follow-up interviews were not conducted because no participants requested an additional interview. Member checking occurred during and after interviews to ensure the accuracy of information provided by participants. Two participants failed to provide feedback on the written transcripts sent to them. The remaining participants did provide feedback. Only one participant revised the transcript. Once the interview transcript review was complete, an appreciation email was sent within four business days to the participants to thank them for participating in the study.

Data Analysis

The explanation-building analytical technique was the data analysis approach used for the study to evaluate possible links between perceptions of management practices and innovation. In conducting academic research, data analysis is among the essential steps in the research process (Leech and Onwuegbuzie 2008). Data analysis includes "organizing data, immersion in the data, formulating categories and themes, coding the data interpreting through analytic memos, defining alternate understandings, and writing the report" (Marshall et al. 2013, 209). Researchers should have an essential concept guide to develop an understanding of data collection and analysis (Marshall et al. 2013).

Data preparation. Before analyzing the data, the transcripts from the interviews were arranged in a usable format and stripped of personal identifiers. According to Golding (2009), researchers should follow the required process to organize and store data. The transcripts were also formatted to support manual and computer-assisted coding.

Data review and coding. The data review process involved listening to and reading through the data. The process of data analysis started by cautiously reading the transcribed text line by line to identify blocks of text that could be categorized and described in a meaningful way. Patterns and meanings were searched for within from the data. In conducting data analysis, Golding (2009) recommended that researchers should familiarize themselves with the data before starting the analysis. Different-colored highlighting pens were used to track the data analysis process. Each audio-recorded interview was listened to twice during the transcription process. Dragon NaturallySpeaking software and Express Scribe transcription software were used to transcribe the audio-recorded interviews.

A coding process similar to a file format was used to organize the transcribed data. Ganapathy (2016) referred to coding as a process of creating the segments of data using category titles or meaningful terms. In conducting qualitative research, Seers (2012) stated that the qualitative data "often takes the form of words or text and can include images" (2). Seers's example was followed regarding sorting data, organizing it, and coding it in a particular format.

After identifying critical blocks of text, the process of creating original codes commenced. The transcribed data was read, line by line, separated into important analytical themes and coded into subcategories by segment, to formalize the data into categories. For example, if a participant shared three ideas, including initiating new ideas, managing new ideas, and sharing new ideas, the codes for these paragraphs could be (a) launch new ideas, (b) manage new ideas, and (c) share new thoughts. The data were manually coded by highlighting the transcripts to note potential patterns.

Analysis of the data. According to Ganapathy (2016), the data analysis process consists of "identifying and locating raw data, structuring raw data, indexing themes, indexing content, extracting content, and searching for a pattern in the data, integrating patterns and coding" (107). In line with Sutton and Austin (2015), concerns, differences, and similarities were identified that emerged from the participants' interview responses.

Relevant themes were identified and examined. Each theme was checked and compared to the other themes established during the data analysis process. In line with Thomas (2006), the findings from the study emerged from the significant ideas in the transcribed data. Each theme was evaluated to validate conclusions and interpret study data.

A detailed analysis of individual themes was reported and evaluated regarding how these themes aligned with the research question. Aligned with Braun and Clarke (2006), each theme was reviewed to determine which items reflected which overarching theme. A report was generated for analysis that had a concise and vivid view of the study findings examples.

Data interpretation in a qualitative inquiry enhances understanding of the topic under investigation and challenges the researcher to question personal assumptions and beliefs (Bloomberg and Volpe 2008). In conducting data analysis, Bowen (2010) suggested the data interpretation process allows a researcher to attach importance to findings, make sense of the results, and reflect on various meanings to present potential explanations and conclusions. In this process, an interpretative reading of data was performed to construct a version of what the data represented. Throughout the process, the focus was on discovering meaning beyond the data details, sorted to arrive at a new understanding.

Data from the transcripts were hand-coded before NVivo 12 Pro was used to identify themes and to manage the transcripts, which were compared to the hand-coded data. NVivo 12 Pro coded and categorized the data collected during interviews with NVivo 12 Pro's text-mining function (Leech and Onwuegbuzie 2008). With the NVivo 12 Pro automated process, themes were identified by analyzing words in the text. NVivo 12 Pro text mining focuses on specific words in the document (Leech and Onwuegbuzie 2008). The search tools in NVivo 12 Pro allowed data investigation at various levels. The coding process was repeated, and the transcripts were reviewed for concerns, differences, and similarities as purported by Sutton and Austin (2015). Coding and themes assisted in presenting study reports and findings.

Memoing Journal

Journal notes were kept throughout the data collection process; these notes were central to the investigation. The memoing journal paved the way to create categories based on the information found in the data recorded in the journals.

Following is an extract from the journal developed during the research process:

> I contacted a participant today, to remind the participant about the forthcoming telephonic interview scheduled for tomorrow between 4:30 p.m. and 5:15 p.m. We have decided that the interview should be rescheduled for next week on the same day and time. Due to bad weather in the location of the participant, communication was poor. I hope the weather improves, and the participant is available for the interview next week.

In conducting the exploratory qualitative research, researchers use the memoing process to perform various actions, such as to map research activities, find meaning from the data, sustain momentum, and develop communication lines (Birks, Chapman, and Francis 2008). The memoing approach is the "storehouse of analytic ideas" (Beck, Moser, and Tscheligi 2014, 2). The memoing process was used to initiate and maintain productivity during the research process and to record conversations and new thoughts that guided the research process. The memoing process helped track and discern what the data indicated. As a result, essential ideas emerged from the data and were interpreted accordingly. In conducting qualitative research, Birks et al. (2008) explained that researchers who use the memoing process engage more thoroughly in the investigation.

Instruments

As the primary instrument for data collection, I observed and viewed participants' experience from their point of view, which technique is supported by Marshall et al. (2013). Qualitative researchers rely on various forms of instruments to gather data, such as interviews, document analysis, and field observations (Chenail 2011). The section includes a description of the various tools used in the study.

The Role of the Researcher

I was the primary instrument responsible for collecting data for the exploratory study, and I was aware of personal identity, assumptions, and biases that, as indicated by

Marshall et al. (2013), could influence the phenomena under study. During this process, several interviews were conducted, and information was gathered that elucidated the topic under study (Barrett 2007) from participants' lived experience. The study on management practices and innovation was subjected to personal biases as I hold a managerial position in an SME and have twelve years of experience working with a variety of teams on strategy implementation. I have interacted directly with various SME middle managers on strategic concerns that improved how value is delivered to customers, and I have had positive and negative experiences working with SME managers. Despite biases in organizations about SME middle managers, they were the focus of the study. Often, middle managers are valuable to work with because of their capabilities and inventive work standards and practices. It can also be challenging to work with them, based on personal experience. As suggested by Sutton and Austin (2015), researchers should proceed in their studies by acknowledging that their expertise and position on the topic of research exerts a significant influence on the review.

Bracketing was incorporated into the study. Bracketing involves self-reflection such that a researcher works to suppress his or her own biases and knowledge regarding the phenomena under study (Tufford and Newman 2010). The tactic of reflexivity helps researchers address experiences, assumptions, and emerging ideas in the research process (Zitomer and Goodwin 2014). Bracketing was used to identify preconceptions and biases. For example, I reflected on my involvement with the data to recognize prejudices as suggested by Tufford and Newman (2010), and I used a journal to record biases during the study process as specified by Cope (2014); the journal helped me remain mindful of potential biases so I could work to prevent them from influencing the process of data analysis. Journals were considered a data source for the research but were used only to identify possible biases that may have arisen during the study. Additional discussion with participants was not initiated, to address potential biases during the study process. Information was not altered, allowing the reporting of accurate findings.

Guiding Interview Questions

The selected interview technique for the exploratory qualitative research study inquiry was semistructured telephonic interviews (see table 1). A semistructured interview is a technique used by qualitative researchers to aid in eliciting facts and knowledge about the phenomenon under study (Mojtahed et al. 2014). The semistructured interview technique facilitated the conversational flow of information, providing the researcher access to additional information and providing participants the opportunity to freely share their experiences, which aligned with advice from

Mojtahed et al. (2014). The interview was conducted telephonically on the date and time agreed. An interpretative analysis was used to determine relationships between theoretical concepts and specific topics that emerged from participants' responses. Interpretative analysis helps researchers understand how study participants describe their experiences (Back et al. 2014).

Table 1. Interview protocol

Interview question number	Research questions
Q1	As a manager in the construction industry, describe, to the best of your ability, certain specific management practices and innovation you have initiated that have created real value for your organization.
	❖ Could you describe further how you think your management practices correlate with your innovation?
	❖ Describe how you think your management practices incentivize and support employees, general monitor performance, and achieve overall business goals.
Q2	Describe your management practices you believe that give your organization an edge over others in the increasingly competitive construction industry of today.
Q3	In the light of what you have done in the past and the current standing of your organization, what would you do differently today regarding your management practices and innovation?

Ethical Considerations

In conducting the exploratory qualitative research, protecting research participants was the central concern. Ethical concerns were addressed in the interest of study participants. For example, confidentiality measures were employed to safeguard participants, and data were transcribed anonymously. Further, the study process was transparent throughout regarding data usage, data analysis, and data storage to help build trust with study participants. According to Sandelowski (2015) and Tracy (2010), ethical considerations should include the procedures used to conduct interviews, overall research conduct, information sharing, and data storage and destruction. To guide the discussion under ethical considerations, the focus was on three primary ethical elements according to the *Belmont Report*: respect for persons, beneficence, and justice (US Department of Health and Human Services 2014).

Respect for Persons

In this research, respect for individuals was paramount. Respect for persons involves valuing and protecting a participant's autonomy and independence to volunteer freely (Ybarra et al. 2016). Participation in the study was voluntary, and participants could withdraw at any time without any consequences. The partnership centered on the informed consent form and interview protocol. Participants' rights, dignity, and safety were secured because each participant had value, and this value guided interactions with participants during interviews. Also, the value of each participant's autonomy and his or her ability to make independent decisions regarding participation in the study was valued. Any needs that arose during the study were addressed, such as answering participants' questions. Participants were provided with contact information if they wanted to communicate before or after the interviews.

Beneficence

Protecting the privacy and confidentiality of participants was required in the study. Beneficence involves the researcher's ability not to harm, to maximize potential benefits, and to minimize probable harm (Ybarra et al. 2016). Also, beneficence describes the researcher's responsibility "to protect the well-being of human participants, not only by minimizing risks of harm to the participant but also by maximizing any potential benefits to the participant" (Ross et al. 2018, 139). The US Department of Health and Human Services (2014) guidelines were followed regarding the principle that research must cause no harm to participants or the general public. The interest of participants was identified as they actively engaged in the study. The study posed only minimal risks.

Justice

Participant selection was carefully considered to ensure that the target population was not selected based on easy accessibility. Justice entails that communities benefit from the outcome of research (Ybarra et al. 2016). Justice requires the "need for equitable distribution of the benefits and burdens of research on humans" (Ross et al. 2018, 139). Participants were selected based on the anticipated study results. Personal biases about the topic under investigation were set aside through memoing.

Summary

Chapter 3 began with a description of the purpose of the study: to explore the constructs of OIT to determine how middle managers may contribute to innovations in the construction industry SMEs. The chapters included a description of the research question and research design, the target population, and the sample. Finally, the procedure, instruments, and ethical considerations were presented. Chapter 4 includes information about the role of the researcher, a description of participants, the research methodology, data analysis, presentation of the data, and the results of the investigation.

RESULTS

Chapter 4 includes the presentation of participants' demographics, the role of the researcher and the potential bias in the study, a presentation of the results, and an evaluation of the findings. The purpose of the exploratory qualitative research was to add to the existing literature on management practices and innovation by exploring the experiences of construction industry SME middle managers with management practices that may facilitate innovation. Given the methodological nature of thematic data analysis, the detailed processes are presented regarding the identification of thematic labels. Specific themes using thematic analysis were uncovered from remarks made by the participants that are relevant in answering the research question: What roles do management practices have in innovation in US SMEs in the construction industry? The chapter comprises five sections: a description of the study and the researcher, a description of the sample, the research methodology as applied to the data analysis, the presentation of data and results, and a summary to conclude the chapter.

Introduction: The Study and the Researcher

The phenomenon was explored by answering the central question: What roles do management practices have in innovation in US SMEs in the construction industry? OIT constructs were intended to provide links between management practices and innovation in SMEs that facilitate economic growth (Karadag 2015) to improve growth and innovation in the construction industry. Understanding qualitative links between management practices and innovation validates previous recommendations concerning the importance of collaboration with partners and networks to innovate (Azadegan 2011; Malmström et al. 2013; Wagner 2012). The analytical approach used in the qualitative inquiry was thematic analysis, which was used to interpret the data through data reduction and to understand the fundamental concepts behind the participants' responses, supported by Corbin and Strauss (2015). Thematic analysis was appropriate in analyzing participants' answers to open-ended questions collected from semistructured interviews as suggested by Clarke and Braun (2017).

Role of the Researcher

As a researcher who had a managerial position in an SME and who has twelve years of experience working with a variety of teams on strategy implementation, I am well-placed to critically infer the complex relations of management practices and innovation in the construction industry. As a strategist, I had direct interaction with various SME middle managers on strategic concerns that improved how companies deliver value to customers. I have had both positive and negative experiences working with SME managers. My working knowledge and skills put me in the best position to clarify significant practices that a middle manager may or may not have experienced in his or her organization.

As an SME manager, one of my biases is the belief that SME managers have innate inventive work standards and practices because of business pressures directing them to complete projects within contract guidelines. Companies have the primary method of engaging in professional networks that allow them to source external resources for joint or single project undertakings. Negative bias in this sample group was that these SME managers are the most challenging group of professionals to work with, as a company can be of poor quality in project dealings.

With these biases, bracketing was implemented, using self-reflection on the topic to suppress bias from the entirety of the data analysis as suggested by Tufford and Newman (2010). These biases provided the opportunity to seek clarification, particularly in topics with personal preconceptions. Documenting personal biases in a journal was necessary. Journals were a data source for the research but were used only to identify possible biases that may have occurred during the study. Although biases were instrumental in posing clarifications, these were not used to initiate a persuasive discussion with participants.

Description of the Sample

Demographic questions were incorporated that identified individuals in the study sample to characterize participants by way of measurable details. These demographic indicators included gender, ethnicity, and years of experience in the construction industry. The demographic data were collected for descriptive purposes only. An analysis of the results by demographic demarcation was outside the scope of the study. Table 2 presents the study participants' demographic characteristics.

Table 2. Gender, race, and years of industry experience

Demographic	*f*	%
Gender	12	
Male	8	66.60
Female	4	33.30
Ethnicity	12	
Caucasian	5	41.60
African American	4	33.30
Hispanic	2	16.60
Others	1	0.08
Years of experience	12	
5 years and below	2	16.60
6 to 10 years	3	25.00
11 years and above	7	58.30

The construction industry is known to be male-dominated (Wright 2014). The data collection reflected this leaning as most of the respondents were men (66.67 percent). Male respondents tended to have eleven or more years of experience, whereas women's experience ranged in the six-to-ten-year category. Table 3 includes a comparison of participants' genders and years of experience in the industry.

Table 3. Cross-tabulated gender and years of experience (*N* = 12)

	Years of experience		
	0–5%	6–10%	11+%
Gender			
Male	8.33	25	33.33
Female	8.33	16.67	8.33

Research Methodology Applied to the Data Analysis

The generic exploratory methodology was followed to conduct the research. Specifically, the explanation-building analytical technique described by Yin (2011) allowed exploration of the attitudes and experiences of participants. According to Percy et al. (2015), generic qualitative research allows researchers to explore "people's attitudes, opinions, or beliefs about a particular issue or experience" (76). Generic qualitative research provides researchers the opportunity to create a research design that blends with their epistemological point of view, specialty, and research questions (Kahlke 2014) without following the main qualitative methodologies.

The generic qualitative method was appropriate to answer the research questions as the study was intended to determine links between management practices and innovation in the context of construction industry SMEs, uncovering the perspectives of twelve middle managers employed in companies across the United States through explanation building and categorization of themes from the semistructured interviews. The exploratory qualitative research offered the chance to discover the point of view of people and their experiences (Percy et al. 2015). Furthermore, the approach led to the discovery of middle managers' perceptions regarding how their management practices contributed to innovation. After the first seven interviews, initial data analysis began.

Dragon NaturallySpeaking Premium and Express Scribe Pro transcription software were both used to transcribe the audio-recorded interviews. Before using the transcription software, I listened to each audio-recorded interview twice. I continued listening during the transcription process. Listening to the audio-recorded interviews allowed me to experience the interview again, which aided in recalling the words participants uttered that were unclear in the audio files.

The semistructured interviews were transcribed within seven days of each interview. The transcripts were emailed to each participant for review within ten business days. The data analysis procedures involved explanation building, an iterative process of pattern matching, to describe how or why the phenomenon occurred (Yin 2011). Data analysis began by cautiously reading the transcribed texts, line by line, to discern blocks of text that could be categorized and described in a meaningful way, based on initial predictions formed from the literature review. Observation notes were made using colored pens near responses where the experience context required further understanding. An example of this situation related to market competition and services provided by participants.

The transcribed data were hand-coded, and possible patterns were noted before uploading the data files generated from the interview transcripts into NVivo 12 Pro qualitative software. Hand-coding was accomplished by reviewing and coding the transcripts as they were read line by line. Seers's (2012) example was followed regarding sorting, organizing, and coding data in a specific format. Identification of critical blocks of text and labeling these texts are both necessary for the creation of original codes. To acknowledge the sensitivity of idea segmentation, shared and new ideas were correctly labeled to distinguish the origination of a unique view.

The coding process using NVivo 12 Pro is cyclical. Whether the codes were meaningful and relevant to the research questions was determined, and coding tags were used to describe the experience associated with the codes. The process aided in determining redundant codes and categorizing codes into a broader category. Using NVivo 12 Pro software enabled the identification of the parent and child nodes used to classify the study themes.

Terms used by participants to answer the interview questions were retained. Saldaña's (2009) coding manual for qualitative researchers defines in vivo coding as a means of allotting labels to a specific part of data using words or phrases correctly. An example is the word *control* to code the phrase "I control the cost of these projects" from the prompt "As a manager in a construction industry, describe, to the best of your ability, certain specific management practices and innovation you have initiated that have created real value for your organization." The coding practice was relevant to the language participants used.

The coding process offered sixty-three in vivo codes reflecting participants' views about valuable management practices and the innovation that participants initiated in their respective organizations. A total of seventy-two in vivo codes emerged in the process. The third interview question generated twenty-five in vivo codes reflecting practices participants could have adopted. These codes formalized these chunks of data into categories under thematic labels. Themes were developed to describe the data. Data were clustered into codes with similar meanings, using memoranda that summarized the code content and assigned thematic labels.

The in vivo codes were reprocessed to determine study themes emerging from coding patterns. Reprocessing involved comparing codes against initial predictions emerging from the literature review. Initially, I predicted that participants would mention innovation in association with good management practices. Participants did not explicitly say *innovation*. Based on participants' verbatim statements focusing on improvement and other effective management practices, two themes emerged in the analysis: improving project management and employing effective practices in managing the competitive construction industry.

In identifying the first theme, the word *innovation* was not well articulated in interviews. Participants were responsive to describing specific practices that brought performance and success to their companies. Participants referred to improvements in project management using keywords *performance* and *success*. Hence, the theme of improving project management emerged.

Participant responses were cross-validated to generate the second theme, with interview question 3: "What would you do differently today regarding your management practices and innovation?" The theme emerged after linking the relationship of improved firm performance with innovation. Participants repeatedly mentioned their learned strategies, and their implementation of technology and software, that improved their overall productivity. The theme of enhancing competitive performance emerged. The themes and subthemes are presented in the next section, along with a narrative to support the findings, including quotations and excerpts from the data, offered as evidence in this investigation.

Presentation of Data and Results of the Analysis

The analysis began by understanding the individual situation of participants in their respective organizations. Participants answered the three main interview questions focusing on management practices with organizational innovation. The purpose of this section is to describe the individual organizational situation of each participant concerning management practices and innovation and then present themes emerging from the analysis of the twelve transcripts.

Analysis by Participant

This subsection contains a discussion of each participant's qualitative experience concerning management practices that facilitate innovation. The goal was to contextualize the situation of each participant and to discover how these situations contributed to the emerging themes. The situational context of each participant was articulated before determining the study themes. Table 4 shows the demographics of each participant.

Table 4. Summary of participants' demographics

Participant code	Gender	Ethnicity	Years of experience
P01	Male	Caucasian	15
P02	Female	Caucasian	6
P03	Male	Latino	12
P04	Male	Caucasian	8
P05	Male	Caucasian - Irish	25
P06	Male	Caucasian	20
P07	Male	African American	20
P08	Female	African American	20
P09	Male	African American	5
P10	Male	Latino	16
P11	Female	Caucasian	6
P12	Female	African American	5

Participant 01 (P01). P01 is a Caucasian male manager with fifteen years of experience working in the construction business. The audio-recorded interview with P01 concluded in forty minutes. P01 used the term *oversee* to describe his management responsibility in "quality improvement, construction safety improvement, technology improvement, project improvement, [and] cost and time saving regarding ongoing projects." Concerning people management, P01 mentioned the word *motivation* to describe how he promotes joint ventures of workers and subcontractors "in various projects that yielded reasonable profits to my organization." P01 considered the people he supervised as collaborators in project expansion and development where projects come from endorsements through various networks. P01 is a businessman who trusted the creativity of people and the intellectual production people could contribute to the company. He further mentioned: "I also created a friendly work climate and environment where workers are encouraged to bring new ideas that help serve our customers."

With new ideas and potential project expansion, P01 "initiated processes and ideas that helped provide capital and funding for new projects." P01 confessed that few of his project explorations had been subjected to testing or simulation to determine feasibility and success. P01 shared that some of his innovation experience was unsuccessful because the concept was an imitated idea that was inappropriate to meet clients' requirements. He stressed the importance of a feasibility study that tests for desirability on whether the innovation is nice to have or is mandatory for the customer. P01 believed that a feasibility study also determines the operational capabilities required for the innovation to be adopted. Although P01 claimed that availability of organizational resources was not an issue in organizational innovation, P01 could not further articulate his internal assessment of the strengths and limitations of the organization's technology, financials, branding, customer service, and partnerships, among other considerations, in the development and adoption of innovation. P01 could only articulate that the issue in matters concerning innovation was "developing the product to suit our client requirement[s] and regulations."

P01 considered the supplier as the organization's "major network." He described suppliers as partners who have the "information necessary to serve our customers." His view about competition in the construction industry requires "effective leadership, knowledge exchange, sustainability, and being able to manage available resources, especially manpower." He considered collaboration with partners "an advantage in meeting goals," which "then increases our productivity and [allows us to] complete projects on time." P01 emphasized putting limitations on the partnership to "avoid trading our advantage away." He considered the management of external knowledge and engagement in partnership in the early stage of the project cycle critical to enhancing product trends.

Participant 02 (P02). P02 is a Caucasian female manager who had worked in the industry for six years. The audio-recorded interview concluded in forty-five minutes. P02 considered new project scheduling tools to be a necessary management practice and innovation that created value for her organization. Project scheduling tracks essential aspects of project coverage, finances, work, and what people need to do to catch up with project deadlines. The detailed schedules track the project key performance indicators, which provide accurate information on physical project accomplishments rather than project plans. Possessing key performance indicators allows a realistic assessment of a project's status. Although P02 valued the importance of project scheduling to innovation, she considered her company to be "old school," only using Microsoft Excel rather than project management software. She justified that the company is small with "no multimillion-dollar projects."

When asked about the specific management practices that influence innovation, P02 was quick to say that a small company requires consultants to "be able to handle our large volume of projects and also the timelines." As a manager, her role was to ensure that consultants were qualified and that they performed the required tasks. She said: "I just try to make sure everyone is on top of everything and everyone's communicating, so there are no missed aspects of the project." She further described that their company has been engaging the services of subcontractors for projects that the company is unable to handle. She claimed that finding and keeping qualified subcontractors is difficult because of strong personalities and tedious work requirements.

P02 related the company's success to their ability to organize projects effectively and efficiently, coupled with goal-driven hard workers and the positive attitude of employees and management. P02 also stressed the positive relationship participants developed with the government as an important factor in becoming competitive in project acquisition. P02 said: "I think the other companies do not have that, and it definitely helps to have a good relationship with them with our projects." When asked about the management practices that could be worked differently to achieve further organizational success, P02 shared that excellent relationships, better communication, and better project management software are essential to productivity. She confided that her boss had high expectations, had less effective communication skills, and refused to invest in better project management software, which made it difficult for her to manage the company effectively.

Participant 03 (P03). P03 is a male Latino manager of a plumbing and heating firm with more than twelve years of working experience. The telephonic interview required forty-five minutes. P03 mentioned that the company initiated the use of technology when he undertook the management of the organization. P03 said that the incorporation of technology accompanies the full streamlining of processes to improve workflow.

For instance, he uses the iPad for communication, GPS, product research, product demonstration, and storage of learning materials. With this innovation, P03 described the positive change as follows: "All of these things have saved us so much time, and they've saved us so much energy and effort and cost savings, and the efficiency has been just phenomenal."

Innovation also improves company productivity in project delivery. P03 shared that he uses his iPad to research the model and serial numbers of equipment instantaneously. He said: "The value of making corrections immediately rather than delaying them is a lot better." He further shared,

> Everybody's attitude is a lot better about it. They feel like they're a little bit more autonomous because they have the power to make better choices because they have a tool in their hands that can help them do that. Reaching out to us is a lot easier.

The achievement made the company decide to explore the use of "slide credit cards in the field too[,] instead of having that step done in the office." P03 claimed that using this technology is efficient and effective in eliminating security costs and data retention needs. He further commented: "There have been a lot of things like that that are just getting better and better all the time."

P03 shared significant information technology improvement; for example, their website assisted them in improving their client relationships, sales productivity, and management procedures. Technology helped the organization to control and manage negative feedback. He believed that "reputation management is huge for small businesses." P03 linked organizational success to the smart implementation of technology. He realized that "we're not super early adopters." P03 is now considering attending conferences and participating in business networks to leverage the capacity to establish partnerships and innovation. P03 said the company was also cautious in adopting innovations because technology has benefits and drawbacks. He said: "I've seen companies buy tons of technology [and] roll it out, only to find out that it didn't work for their company[, so they] had to roll it back and wasted tons of money."

In consolidating the organizational priorities of management practices and innovation, P03 said the company focused "on improving the efficiency." He prided himself on success by describing asset growth:

> We've grown in the past fourteen years by about $2.5 million a year .... So, we've roughly doubled the amount of work we're doing, which is excellent, and we're doing it with only, I want to say[,] maybe three or four more technicians than we had when we started.

P03 related the intention to use technology as the most influential factor in their success. P03 said: "We've done that by being more efficient." The second factor was his work attitude, such as "being firm and fair as well as friendly." Being fair means distributing the work to a qualified person in the nearest service area. He shared that ensuring the highest efficiency "helps whittle down unnecessary expenditures. It improves productivity and improves our profit and our bottom line."

The third factor he shared was ensuring technicians were provided professional development. He said, "We go ahead and send them to go and put that training into use, and then [we] watch them knock it out of the park." The company also provides in-house training at various levels. The company evaluates learning outcomes based on real work scenarios. The training is similar when implementing new technology. He considered training and instantaneous learning as central to the acquisition of knowledge. He said that "the ability to do that in real time when it's fresh in [the employee's] mind is huge."

Participant 04 (P04). P04 is a Caucasian male manager with eight years of working experience in the construction industry. The interview lasted forty-five minutes. P04 considered the establishment of safety rules and measured an accomplishment that created value to the organization. P04 said that to maintain a competitive edge in the construction industry, the management should see ideas differently and change old ways of doing business. With the rising interest in safety in the workplace, the management of any construction firm should understand that well-organized safety measures afford firms a viable competitive advantage. P04 believed the organizational value of safety regulations as a management style is gradually shifting to be more visionary, innovative, and responsive to workers' needs. P04 is among the businesspeople who perceive employees as viable resources in achieving organizational goals.

P04 shared that his managerial responsibilities include working with subcontractors and investors who share external funding with the intention of making a profit. P04 believed that exploring new ideas in a meaningful manner is central for companies to improve their processes, bring new products or services to the marketplace, and strengthen productivity and presence in the market. P04 is among the business managers who recognized that the construction industry market is becoming highly competitive. He shared the following:

> These parties invest resources more on external knowledge, especially to initiate a new idea in complex projects[,] because they want to be successful. I have worked with contractors who are more interested in automation and constantly improving product because of market competition.

P04 shared evidence of how quick access to the internet and know-how has increased competition and opportunities for companies to collaborate and share knowledge.

P04 acknowledged that the industry is facing stout competition. He believed that "commitment of our leadership and management" is the key driving their success. P04 described the management team as "cooperative" with an emphasis on rewarding the hard work of employees and ensuring the involvement of contractors "at the beginning of new projects." P04 also stated that "shared and managed knowledge and information" through their training policy gave them the edge to compete in the industry. He also acknowledged innovation and practices that he described as "novel practices" as important in the sustainability of operations. He admitted that although the organization is apparently "okay," the company is in "shortage of financial resources to initiate novel practices that can result in product breakthrough." P04 confided the company is considering external resources to fund these breakthroughs. He said: "Maybe seek external collaboration and partnerships."

Participant 05 (P05). P05 is a male Caucasian of Irish descent who has been managing a construction industry firm for twenty-five years. The audio-recorded interview lasted for forty-five minutes. Among study participants, he had seen the most industry evolution. He described these changes: "I don't know what has happened lately in the construction industry. … There are a lot of products now that got developed that are more environmentally friendly than the others." He described his job managing project sourcing, human resources, and projects. His tasks include identifying subcontractors and skilled laborers to work in the completion of detailed work such as plumbing, electrical works, and drywall.

When asked about specific practices that result in innovation, he confided: "I don't actively reach out. This kind of stuff comes up in conversation all the time." He further commented that his forte is in sourcing people who can do the job. P05 is a transactional leader who interacts with employees using the contract employees have signed. He said that when employees do not accomplish what they signed up for, they will not be paid. He shared: "The insulation guys would sign a contract for doing the insulation, so it's up to them to insulate, and if they don't do it, they don't get paid. I'll call on a different person to do it." The same is true for the quality of work. He said he hires inspectors and inspects himself if the work is of quality. He was clear in his policy about work payment. He said: "You just don't get paid. You're told to do it again and again and again."

Reputation matters to P05; "It's usually word of mouth. That's a fact. … With a good reputation. I don't have to advertise very much." P05 established his niche in a community surrounded by Irish people and people who have worked with him for twenty-five years. He shared: "And I don't even have a website. I'm Irish, and there are not a lot of Irish people here. We would call some estate agents, developers, stuff like that—people I've been working with for twenty-five years." He termed this practice as *networking*, a term he has used in this context for three decades. He said, "These guys [whom] I [have] know[n] for thirty years, and people that [*sic*] I [have] worked with before like developers, homeowners that [*sic*] we worked with before, a homeowner that [*sic*] knows another homeowner and they recommend my organization." He justified that, unlike working with multimillion-dollar contractors, the network is much more comfortable with services for individual houses. P05 struggled with financial aspects. He claimed that subcontractors who are not doing their jobs and homeowners who keep changing their minds could hurt the company financially.

P05 operates a small yet stable company. He survived for several years in a business where pricing is unpredictable and expensive. Despite this success, he identified the use of "cell phone technology" as an important aspect of the documentation of his operation. He said: "I used to use pen and paper, jotters and notebooks, and ledgers, and things like that. Now I put it all on the computer and save it."

Participant 06 (P06). P06 is a male Caucasian who reported twenty years of managerial experience in the construction business. The telephonic interview concluded in twenty-five minutes. The conversation was interrupted by P06's business partners; therefore, P06 was unable to complete the final interview steps. P06 provided feedback on the interview transcript, offering valuable insight into his organization. P06 shared that studying the project and detailing the activities, including the people who will be hired, is a useful management practice in his organization. He claimed that moving the business forward, understanding the marketplace, and innovating adds value to the organization.

According to P06, being in the business for twenty years has taught him that adapting services or products to the level of the competition is a considerable opportunity a manager should take. With this approach, planning for innovation must be a regular part of the business strategy. P06 is a visionary and a business leader in the industry who survived the market hurdles. His experiences show how innovation improves business survival and how these innovations thrive and drive to increase organizational profits.

P06's experiences in the industry convinced him that the discipline of leaders and the management of people are the building blocks of an innovative organization. He argued that leaders could use existing or even fresh ideas for innovation by developing an environment that explores innovation networks so the company may grow and thrive. Leaders can advance activities that encourage employees to engage in innovation. In such a situation, employees tend to know that they are valuable resources and are permitted to share meaningful ideas. P06 believed that when leadership is on top and ahead of everything, "time is not wasted at all."

P06 instilled a culture of innovation by ensuring employee engagement in project activities. An example of this daily activity included organizing meetings to orient team members. He emphasized the daily interactions with the team when he rolled up project activities, ensuring that team members have an equal understanding. He said,

> I have to make sure [that] every day I walk them through it. At the site meetings, daily meetings, and orientation, we refresh every part of what needs to be done on a particular day and to make them expect … to make them know the expectation on that very day.

He considered that these meetings set the expectations for the work everyone must accomplish. He observed that this practice had made a "very positive ending. … Success is expected at the end, daily, and of course overall at the end of that project."

The second practice he adopted in the organization was to provide transportation for his employees to arrive at work on time. Providing transportation gave employees the impression that time is valuable for management. He stressed: "I show them by picking them up, or that timely manner is important. They see that it gets into them. And they so appreciate that they don't like to play with any time of the management."

Participant 07 (P07). P07 is an African American manager of a construction company with twenty years of experience in the industry. A telephonic interview lasted for thirty-five minutes. P07 owned a construction business that was no longer in operation before his current position as a construction manager. P07 said that his past experiences as a business owner helped him fulfill his present responsibilities as a construction manager. He associated organizational success with efficiency because of the hiring of employees with specialized skills. P07 is among the leaders who viewed skilled workers as a necessity. As markets shift and competition increases, productivity and worker efficiency are becoming even more critical to profits. With skilled workers, P07 believed he could provide specialized services for customers who are more particular about spending money on quality services. Hiring skilled workers assured him that his company's services could remain competitive.

However, P07 noted that this practice is more expensive than employing the skilled generalist worker. Hiring specialists assured him the work would be completed on schedule. He justified, "Many times I found myself redoing work I had paid someone else to do to make a deadline." He admitted that the downside of hiring skilled workers is obtaining loyalty from these people toward the company. His observations and experiences in using this hiring strategy are consistent with most companies that were forced to run lean because of the lack of availability of loyal employees.

Among the business influences of contracting with skilled workers was the management of cash flow. P07 said, "In a contract-out business with daily overhead cost, management of cash flow is challenging." He further described this situation: "Paying workers by the day helped to complete projects, but it made it extremely difficult to manage cash flow on a day-to-day basis because customers do not pay that way."

Participant 08 (P08). P08 is a female African American manager who reported twenty years of working experience in the construction company. P08's interview lasted forty minutes. She described herself as having had "a successful business for more than twenty years." As a woman working in an industry dominated by men, P08 confided that the employees are her family. She believed that when workers understand that the organization values them, they do better and appreciate the organization. Such workers are happy with their jobs and are productive. P08 believed that treating her employees as family motivates them and encourages them to stay with the company. With her strategy, P08 does not need to deal with hiring and training new employees.

P08 claimed that treating employees like family created a positive work atmosphere. She related that when employees feel valued as more than just productivity machines, they become more motivated. P08 said, "When workers are home at work, they become committed [and] loyal and [they] develop the inner drive for creativity and productivity."

However, she said that adopting this management practice has its disadvantages. She realized that in a competitive industry, the provision of employees' paid benefits does not matter for skilled workers who want higher pay for the job. She said, "I still lost some of my most talented people to other projects because they didn't value having company-paid benefits and opted to go with companies that would pay them more." Also, she claimed, "A lot of family issues found their way into the workplace, and it caused delays on projects."

P08's strategies showed evidence that leading the company like a family provides advantages and disadvantages. She had more engaged productive employees and considered the cost associated with paying benefits for employees who may have personal issues that could affect the company's productivity. Despite ways to manage the disadvantages, such as ways to use other related management systems, P08 considered her management style best. She believed these practices are the reason for her longevity in the business.

Participant 09 (P09). P09 is an African American male manager with five years of working experience in the construction industry. Before his position as construction manager, P09 owned a construction business that he sold, because of an injury that prevented him from working for more than a year. P09 shared, "I was later hired to work as a manager by my former senior staff who took over the business when I sold it." As a manager, he believed employees' loyalty is essential for business success. He expected an emotionally connected employee to stay with the company, even when other employers offer higher salaries, more training, and benefits.

P09 shared that with fair treatment from leaders, a loyal employee is the most engaged and productive. He described his leadership behaviors as "firm and fair." He considered these behaviors as his style of improving employees' loyalty. He ensures that employees' skills are appreciated by making their role a significant part of the organization.

P09 shared the depressed economic situation in his geographic area, which made the hiring activities of skilled and experienced workers possible. With the rising competition of hiring skilled workers in an extremely scarce skilled labor workforce, leaders can only rely on their pool of loyal, qualified employees. P09 claimed that a caring leader who listens and appreciates suggestions from employees could develop trust and respect, which empowers and motivates employees to do their share in terms of organizational productivity. Acknowledging competition in the industry, P09 shared that quality work from the skilled worker, fair wages, and employment stability are the management practices that gave the business its success. Although he considered his business venture a success, he admitted that he lacks strategic planning in leadership sustainability. The telephonic interview ended in thirty minutes.

Participant 10 (P10). P10 is a Latino male manager with sixteen years of working experience serving homeowners in the repair and building maintenance field. The telephonic interview with P10 lasted forty-five minutes. Unlike other participants in the study, P10 emphasized work processes, including materials used, as valuable for the organization. For him, the use of innovative chemicals in cleaning is cost-effective and efficient. He said, "It minimizes our time, but it maximizes our efficiency."

P10 described a company with a casual process. He offered an experience where he does the supervision, as well as the cleaning work along with other cleaning staff. He shared this experience:

> On our large houses, we'll have four to five people. And I'm a leader. I take charge of the team. So of course, I'm in the house, working on the house at the same time. But now and then I'll get off the ladder, I'll come out of the room, and I'll check on where everybody's at. So, it's me just going to them and talking to them and always having a sense of where they are.

In his words, the only time employees used cell phone technology was with a client who has a huge mansion. He said,

There have only been a couple of times we've been in a house so big where we've needed to get on the phone with each other and find out where each other are … easy to keep track of, and everybody follows the plan that I put in place.

When asked about management practices that encourage employees' commitment to quality services, P10 underlined the culture of giving a tip, which their satisfied customers practiced. P10 shared that the company monitors customers' tips and uses this information to improve the quality of service they provide. He described this instance:

So, I have on record this house has tipped us this much before, or my boss does. He says, "Hey, this house is a big tipper. This house is a small tipper. Let's see if we can improve it, so we know what to expect." The bar is set.

Excellent and exclusive connection with the chemical supplier has been pointed out as the primary factor driving the success of the company. P10 shared that the company offers services that other competitors could not provide. P10 said: "My boss has connections with the pool industry. Like, we don't just do windows; we also treat houses. Whole houses we clean on the outside, and we clean roofs, siding, sidewalks, and ev [sic] if they ask us to. The chemical that we use for that is stronger than what any regular person can go and get because we get it custom ordered through a pool company that [says] they use this stuff to treat pools. We get it directly from the source, and [we do] with the TG-4 that we use. We get a specialty one that nobody else in the area has the connection to."

He described this competitive advantage as "dominant control" over the services in three states. Other than the material used in service delivery, P10 shared that the company developed an effective method of cleaning that has been well adopted by its employees. He shared,

We have a technique how we squeegee and clean the sides of the windows that there are never any streaks as long as you do the technique properly. So, add that to the chemical, and we have a perfect window.

When asked about the technique name, he answered: "My boss came up with this technique, and now we teach it to whoever we employ under us. … It is a process that my boss came up with when he started this company thirty years ago."

Although P10 claimed the company collaborated with other companies, he described these companies as "small, like little mom-and-pop shops, just, you know, a man and a bucket who [*sic*] does it." For some work, the company engaged with subcontractors who could do the work more effectively and efficiently than their workers. P10 was adamant in linking the business success to the chemical company with which they partnered. P10 regretted that the company only maximized this networking opportunity recently. He said: "If we had made that connection a long time ago, or at least reached out and tried to find it, we could have been maximizing our profits a long time ago." P10 said that the company could have researched or networked with like-minded companies to "figure out the right chemical mixture." When asked about the possibility of networking now that the company acknowledges the importance of it, P10 said: "The only other group that was out there that ever gave us any competition … is now out of business because we took over pretty much all of their customers."

Participant 11 (P11). P11 is a Caucasian female manager who described her primary responsibilities as "productivity and quality in existing projects." Other than performing as the cost controller, she is also engaged in ensuring training for employees to meet quality service standards. She shared: "I engage different practices in carrying out my responsibilities, for example, using skills, resources, [and] human capital, which are essential in facilitating how we run our business to maintain market share." Effective resource management was the primary contributor to driving organizational productivity. She explained that these practices "show a relationship [of] how we provide reoccurring services to customers." These practices made her company able to compete in the marketplace. P11 added that offering unique services also "improve[d] productivity [and] lower[ed] cost, [and helped them to] become competitive, develop new market lines, and achieve faster completion of projects." She believed that "understanding how to market or provide novel services can be an important way to innovate."

As novel services are essential to the organization, P11 encouraged their employees "to collaborate with outside sources of information that can help them execute their responsibilities." She shared that to compete in the market, employees earn compensation for bringing new ideas that could improve the business marketability in the community. The level of openness for networking and collaboration gave them more advantages in accessing the market environment. She said: "I have used our network channel to improve profits for my organization, improve our position in the market, and make good returns. We find ways to improve services to our customers when we share resources with others."

Although networking and collaboration have disadvantages like shared risks, this practice often drives returns, as some partners willingly share workforce or other resources that help them execute projects successfully. P11 claimed, "When we find ways to use the ideas shared from our networks, we often solidif[y] our presence in the marketplace." She admitted that with collaboration and networking, the company would need to find "better ways ... to overcome cultural barriers when engaging in joint projects with other organizations and networks." She added that "specific management practices" must be employed for the "dispensation of human capital." Overall, the audio-recorded interview with P11 lasted thirty-five minutes.

Participant 12 (P12). P12 is an African American female manager who had been in the business for at least five years. The interview with P12 continued for forty minutes. Like P11, her responsibilities are managing the "project quality and general productivity, including cost saving and time-saving." She believed that collaboration is effective in tapping human resources and some other resources that other organizations may not have. Openness in managing talents, resources, and finances could leverage the rising demand for market competition. P12 shared that opening the doors for networking with stakeholders and potential business partners could complement and extend core expertise to provide the most efficient and effective means of providing complete service for business clients.

According to P12, collaboration has helped the company "do well[, better] than some of our competition in the business." She further shared that the collaboration resulted in joint investments, risk sharing, and development of "new trade opportunities." P12 described that collaboration is appropriate when entering a new market to "obtain complementary resources that could help us compete in the market." As a manager, she used skilled workers in the company's engagement with outside organizations and networks. Her experiences using this approach had "increased profits and the chances to stay in the market." She reported that the company's return on investment from joint projects was "impressive."

Although P12 shared impressive accomplishments in networking and collaborating with stakeholders in increasing business profitability, she concluded that among the practices she could do differently was to retain "more internal resources to access external resources." Needing internal resources shows that networking and collaboration must also work internally in the organization. Making this role a shared responsibility with other internal stakeholders could further extend the innovation efforts and increase organization profitability. Success in collaboration in the organization requires strong leadership and skilled people who can operate across corporate boundaries. Like P12, employees who could participate in collaboration activities must be culturally savvy and have clear processes for sharing knowledge.

Data Analysis by Theme

The exploratory qualitative research study investigated the links between management practices and innovation to validate previous researchers' recommendations concerning the importance of collaboration with partners and networks to innovate (Azadegan 2011; Dahlborg et al. 2017; Duus and Cooray 2014; Malmström et al. 2013; Wagner 2012). The links were explored to answer the central question: What roles do management practices have in innovation in US SMEs in the construction industry? Two main themes emerged from the twelve study participants' transcripts: improving project management and improving competitive performance. Each common theme was partitioned into subthemes, categorized as management practices and summarized in table 5.

Table 5. Common themes and subthemes

Common themes	Subthemes
Improving project management	Sharing information Bringing new ideas Efficient project management
Improving competitive performance	Effective delivery of service Knowledge exchange and collaboration Effective leadership

Theme 1—Improving project management. Theme 1 was labeled "improving project management" after consolidating participant responses regarding management practices they believed to play a valuable role in innovation. Subthemes are management practices articulated by the participants that had perceived value in innovation, including sharing information, bringing new ideas, and managing projects efficiently.

Sharing of information. The management practice emerged as a subtheme after consolidating input from participants regarding internal and external exchanges of data from and among company employees, subcontractors, suppliers, and other stakeholders. The twelve participants supported this subtheme. P09, for instance, who opted to turn over the leadership to his senior staff because of physical injury, stressed the value of encouraging employees to share their ideas for potential project exploration.

P01 illustrated how these information exchanges within and outside the company work:

> Our major network is our suppliers. We partner with them and share information necessary to serve our customers. I also created a friendly work climate and environment where workers are encouraged to bring new ideas that help serve our customers.

Like P01, P11 also encouraged "collaboration with outside sources of information that can help them execute their responsibilities." The collaboration was even expressed in a company policy that compensates employees who can bring new ideas. P11 had this statement: "They are often told to share new ideas and are compensated when they bring new ideas to the table that helps [*sic*] improve services to the market."

Bringing new ideas, processes, and technology. The subtheme of bringing new ideas, processes, and technology emerged among ten participants in the study who recognized the importance of external resources in business success: subcontractors, suppliers, clients, consultants, and investors. P05, who owned a company for twenty-five years, even recognized that without skilled workers, whom he contracts out for work, he would not be able to sustain his business. P05 shared that he made use of notebooks, jotters, ledgers, and pens for business records in the past, but now he can use the computer to store those records.

These subthemes were also akin to experiences of participants that relate to engaging in different efficient practices, maintaining control over the market because of innovation, and using gadgets and software to improve productivity. P04 shared an experience where contractors equated investment in external knowledge with success. As a young manager, P04 said he had "worked with contractors who are more interested in automation and constantly improving product because of market competition." P11 offered a similar perspective, stating that his company institutionalized employee compensation for bringing new ideas to improve the company's services. P03 realized the importance of implementing new ideas and technology in the overall productivity of his organization. He regretted his inability to integrate smart phone technology sooner in his business. P03 said: "We should have done integrated smart phone three years earlier, at least. We could have been more efficient faster. I'm kicking myself for that every day."

Efficient project management. Efficient project management emerged from participants who described their project roles in ensuring that team members completed the work on time and that it was of quality. P07, who had twelve years of experience, believed the relationship between efficiency and the organization's leaders' ability to recognize individual skills contributed to efficient project management. P07 hired skilled workers to do specialized jobs. The workers of this company are project-based, and he is not obligated to guarantee paid benefits.

Unlike P07, P03 believed that efficiency includes loyal skilled employees, homegrown from their training program. Their training program has been described as instantaneous and is technology-driven. P03 served as the training, monitoring, and evaluation officer for staff whom he found less competent in specific work. P03 improved their training system by issuing training tickets and by training them on-site using technology such as a smart phone and iPad. P03 said:

> We have better oversights [*sic*] of them, and we can measure their schedules more efficiently and manage. If there are corrections that are necessary, we can do those immediately, because we see the ticket, and we're like, "Okay, there's information. We need you to go back and get it right now," instead of having to be like a day later, "Hey, it's not on the ticket. We need to send you back."

P10 described efficiency using the benefits the company got from the chemical mixtures and the cleaning techniques developed over the years. P10 attributed these successes to his boss's networking efforts, working knowledge, and experience. Internally, his boss trained cleaning technicians in the company's in-house technique. He shared: "My boss came up with this technique, and now we teach it to whoever we employ under us." Externally, the owner had a partnership with a chemical company that gave them the exclusive use of an effective cleaning compound. The partnership is considered a company accomplishment, which now has the "dominant control" in the marketplace. P10 further said:

> I found that we can take the same chemical cleaner and wipe it and scrub it that way and then wipe it off with a wet rag and it looks even better than us hosing it down. It minimizes our time, but it maximizes our efficiency.

Theme 2—Improving competitive performance. Organizational performance comprises part of an industry's competitive landscape. In the study, corporate areas that improved the competitive business performance included (a) effective delivery of service, (b) knowledge exchange and collaboration, and (c) effective leadership. The following subthemes are strategies business managers could adapt to compete with the rising demand for innovation:

Effective delivery of service. The first subtheme offered by participants was the effective delivery of services. The twelve study participants maintained that service completion must end on schedule and that work should be finished at minimal cost. These participants offered various project management strategies to achieve a specific job at a desired value and according to a desired timeline. These strategies required project managers to use new software, hire technical staff with expertise, and use various innovative approaches to meet the competitive advantage of firms.

P09, who left the business because of an injury and was rehired, shared that employees receive bonuses for projects that are "under budget or ahead of schedule and [that] still meet our standards." P05, who operates and owns a house repair and maintenance business, cited project schedule, timing, and cost as essential to delivery of service. He said: "I have to schedule [clients] in advance and tell them I can't do [*sic*] for six months because I got someone else. You have to budget these sort of long term." P05 believed that his commitment to finishing the project using different innovative strategies gave him a positive reputation in his community.

P03 related the success of his business to efficiency and the highly skilled workers employed in his company. He described the level of competence as being indebted to the training program he implemented in the organization. Alongside this training program was the provision of technology where he gave instantaneous hands-on training to employees who failed to meet the work standards. P03 stressed that with the incorporation of technology, project delays became controlled.

Like the other female SME managers included in the study, P02 focused on efficient scheduling as a criterion of quality delivery of service. She said: "We monitor by the way the project's going. … If we're missing deadlines, that means we have to do things differently." P02 discussed that management used project reporting as a cue to implement risk mitigation and used coping strategies to "get the workload back to us quicker." She further emphasized that "the goal of the project is to get it built promptly and be under budget as far as how much it's going to cost sales." She explained that when they miss timelines, the financing will incur "big interest rates."

Knowledge exchange and collaboration. Knowledge exchange and collaboration emerged after consolidating patterns of similar words and phrases that describe information and resource sharing and outcomes when these resources are collective. Participants mentioned the exchange of information and collaboration of resources extensively in various topical project management areas such as risk management, human support, finance, and business strategies. The shared information provides managers with better ideas on how to strategically manage projects at the appropriate cost and according to the desired timelines. Collaboration is also essential in meeting project requirements, particularly workforce, financial, and technological resources.

P12, who manages "every activity about project quality and general productivity, including cost saving, and time-saving," said: "Collaborating with other organizations that have manpower and resources that my organization does not have, I believe it has helped us to do well[, better] than some of our competition in the business." P12 claimed that investing in different projects with other organizations could allow her company to share the risks, yet this practice also "develop[s] new trade opportunities."

Like P12, P11 believed that his "ability to use different networks and collaboration in carrying out different projects gave my organization an edge over our competitors that are not in our network." Regardless of organization size, P11 used the availability of collaborative projects to "improve profits for my organization, improve our position in the market, and make good returns." P11 used the phrase "channel network" to indicate sources of information to improve and leverage market competition. He said: "We find ways to improve services to our customers when we share resources with others. We also share risks. Instead of working alone on a project, we collaborate with others, sometimes with those bigger or smaller than my organization."

With collaboration and sharing of information, P11 claimed, ideas and offerings of novel products and services came from the learning opportunities gained from various networks. Learning opportunities gave the organization strategies for "doing things differently" to "improve productivity, lower cost, become competitive, develop new market lines, and achieve faster completion of projects." Innovation for this organization comes from understanding the market and providing new services.

Although P04 acknowledged the importance of innovation, he claimed, with regret, that the organization has a "shortage of financial resources to initiate novel practices that can result in product breakthrough." Collaboration for P04 is essential to support knowledge exchange, which their organization is unable to provide. According to P04, "what we can do differently is to consider external resources, maybe seek external collaboration and partnerships."

Effective leadership. The effective leadership theme emerged from various management practices participants identified, including open collaboration, initiating and imitating new ideas, supporting ideas, embracing technology, providing incentives, mentoring, motivating, and building good rapport. Even though participants did not comprehensively explain a few management practices, these management practices were related to effective leadership, which is described in the subsequent chapter. Although almost every participant claimed leadership is essential to business growth and business sustainability, very few described what effective leadership means in terms of leading a highly competitive industry. Two managers wanted their bosses to establish a good relationship with external partners and use technology to achieve the need for efficient and effective project management.

P10 demonstrated the outcome of proactive leadership in establishing the dominance of their service in the market. P10 claimed that the combined years of experience, an innovative technique in the offered service, and novel products significantly contributed to business success. P10 confided that if connections had been available earlier, his company would have benefited from those connections before now.

P04 described the high-level commitment of leadership and management in knowledge sharing. With eight years of experience, he had seen how the management team had been cooperative in rewarding hard work and how they had involved contractors at the beginning of new projects. His organization offered a training policy that ensured the practical means of "managing knowledge and information effectively."

P01 linked effective leadership to "knowledge exchange, sustainability, and being able to manage available resources, especially manpower." He was one among the twelve participants who demonstrated openness to new ideas outside the organization to compensate for a seeming lack of resources for innovation. Given a chance to manage "external knowledge and information sharing to enhance product trends," P10 shared that engagement of subcontractors should be done earlier in new projects to ensure commitment to organizational changes and development.

Summary

In the exploratory qualitative research study, OIT was used to establish the expertise of SME construction middle managers with management practices that may facilitate innovation and economic growth by answering the research question: What roles do management practices have in innovation in US SMEs in the construction industry? The semistructured interviews with three open-ended questions validated the importance of collaboration with partners and networks to innovate. The thematic results analysis revealed two themes: improving project management and engaging in effective practices in managing the competitive construction industry.

First, improving project management aligned with innovation, perceived to be valuable in the industry. Participants recognized that project management might improve through sharing information, bringing innovative ideas, and managing projects efficiently. Second, participants believed the role of management practices in innovation in US SMEs in the construction industry involved improving competitive performance. Participants' perceived improved performance as affecting the effective delivery of service, knowledge exchange and collaboration, and effective leadership. The themes are further discussed in the subsequent chapter. Chapter 5 also contains a comparison of the findings with the conceptual framework and previous literature, along with limitations of the study and the implications of the findings. Finally, a conclusion will summarize the research.

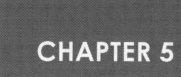

CHAPTER 5

DISCUSSION, IMPLICATIONS, AND RECOMMENDATIONS

Chapter 5 contains a discussion of study results, including a comparison of findings to previous literature and interpretations of findings using the study's theoretical framework as a lens. The chapter also includes limitations, implications of the study, and recommendations for future research. The chapter ends with a conclusion of the complete study.

Summary of the Results

A review of the literature regarding management practices and innovation in SMEs in the construction industry determined a gap in the body of work related to construction industry management practices and innovation in SMEs (Shahbazpour et al. 2015; Yusof et al. 2014). The purpose of the exploratory qualitative research was to add to the existing literature on management practices by exploring the constructs of OIT to determine how middle manager practices facilitate innovations in SMEs in the construction industry. The research question for the study was, What roles do management practices have in innovation in US SMEs in the construction industry?

The research question, investigated through an exploratory qualitative methodology, aimed to determine how middle managers in SMEs in the construction industry may contribute to innovation through management practices. Participants were selected based on the research questions, theoretical perspective, and data informing the research as supported by Sargeant (2012). Semistructured interviews and open-ended questions were used to understand the experiences, perceptions, and attitudes of twelve SME managers concerning management practices that may facilitate innovation. The findings provided insights into the research problem and offered several themes for discussion.

Management practices are essential in any industry, including SMEs, to determine the best practices that enable a firm to survive in a dynamic and uncertain business environment. SMEs play a fundamental role in the US economy because they employ more than 50 percent of the workforce in the private sector (Ilegbinosa and Jumbo 2015). Effective management practices are needed to create innovation in SMEs in construction agencies (Yusof et al. 2014).

The significance of the study relates to the importance and relevance of SMEs. Many SME organizations still find it challenging to attain innovation that leads to growth and stability (Ajayi and Morton 2015). Developing innovation in SMEs has become an interest and a top priority of SME managers to guarantee their continued existence and growth in the economy (Wonglimpiyarat 2015), and innovation is necessary for firms to compete successfully and achieve competitive advantage (Arlbjørn and Paulraj 2013). The findings show the importance of innovation and competitiveness for SMEs.

The study focused on determining the relationship between management practices and innovation in SMEs in the construction industry in the United States, intended to ascertain the essential part that SMEs play in the economy and innovation. The guiding theoretical framework for the research was OIT, which provided a lens (Abouzeedan and Hedner 2012; Chesbrough 2012; Crema et al. 2014; Hossain 2013; Storchevoi 2015) through which to explore management practices and innovation experiences of construction middle managers in SMEs.

Broader-framework settings influence OIT, and open innovation encompasses activities such as search, sourcing, cooperation, and licensing (Herstad et al. 2008), reflected in participants' responses and the themes that emerged. Recent studies perceived open innovation as disseminated practices focused on management of knowledge flow, such as accessing, harnessing, and absorbing the flow of knowledge beyond company boundaries (Chesbrough 2017; West and Bogers 2017), also represented through participants' responses. The theory provided valuable insight into participant responses and the themes that emerged. Thematic analysis revealed two major themes: improving project management and improving competitive performance.

Theme 1: Improving Project Management

SME managers mentioned ways to improve project management, which consisted of three subthemes. Improving project management emerged as the central theme by consolidating three patterns of management practices related to innovation: (a) sharing of information; (b) bringing new ideas, processes, and technology; and (c) managing projects efficiently. Sharing of information emerged as a subtheme regarding internal and external exchanges of information from company employees and among subcontractors, suppliers, and other stakeholders. The twelve participants supported this subtheme. The thought of bringing new ideas, processes, and technology emerged among ten participants who recognized the importance of external resources in business success, which included subcontractors, suppliers, clients, consultants, and investors. Efficient project management emerged from participants who described their project roles in ensuring that team members completed the work on time and that it was of quality.

Theme 2: Improving Competitive Performance

Participants mentioned three effective practices regarding improving competitive performance. Participants articulated practices that were important to the success and longevity of businesses: (a) effective delivery of quality services, (b) knowledge exchange and collaboration, and (c) effective leadership. Effective delivery of service was the first subtheme to emerge. It was mentioned by the twelve participants, who maintained that services must be completed on schedule and work finished at minimal cost.

Knowledge exchange and collaboration emerged after consolidating patterns of similar words and phrases that described information and resource sharing and the outcomes. Participants mentioned the exchange of information and collaboration of resources extensively in various topical project management areas such as risk management, human resources, finances, and business strategies. The effective leadership theme emerged from different management practices mentioned by participants, including being open for collaboration, initiating and imitating new ideas (Grimpe and Sofka 2016), supporting ideas, embracing technology (Drew 2006; Parasuraman 2000), providing incentives, mentoring, motivating, and building good rapport (Arena et al. 2017).

Discussion of the Results

The exploratory qualitative study intended to add to the existing literature on management practices by exploring the constructs of OIT to determine how middle manager practices facilitate innovations in SMEs in the construction industry. The research question for the study was, What roles do management practices have in innovation in US SMEs in the construction industry? Two themes emerged from the thematic analysis: improving project management and improving competitive performance. For improving project management, three subthemes emerged: (a) sharing of information; (b) bringing new ideas, processes, and technology; and (c) managing projects efficiently.

For improving competitive performance, three additional subthemes emerged: (a) effective delivery services of quality services, (b) knowledge exchange and collaboration, and (c) effective leadership. The discussion of the results includes an interpretation of the findings by relating each of the findings to the research question and previous literature. The section also presents the extent to which the findings answered the research question.

Respondents who participated in the study were mostly men (66.67 percent), reflecting the demographics stated in the literature. The construction industry is known to be a male-dominated market (Wright 2014). Although women comprised the minority, years of experience may have had a stronger influence on the results than gender as the research involved effective practices learned over time.

Construction is a unique industry, and managers probably follow similar protocols according to regulations to lead and manage. Participants' years of experience clustered in the ranges of zero to five years, six to ten years, and eleven to twenty-five years. Women tended to have between six and ten years of experience, and men tended to have eleven or more years of experience. Regarding experience, the sample was quite diverse, which provided strength to the study findings as the themes that emerged were prevalent across expertise as well as age. Results also indicated a consensus among participants, as at least ten participants mentioned the subthemes, describing unique problems and solutions in construction and adding to the implications of the results.

Theme 1: Improving Project Management

The SME managers mentioned ways to improve project management that led to three subthemes. As previously mentioned, management practices related to innovation involve sharing of information; bringing new ideas, processes, and technology; and managing projects efficiently. Sharing resources, including data, contributes to effective management practices that would lead to innovation (Crema et al. 2014; Dahlander and Gann 2010). Open innovation entails distributed innovation practices based on managed knowledge flow that involves accessing, harnessing, and absorbing the flow of knowledge beyond companies' boundaries (Chesbrough 2017; West and Bogers 2017). Open innovation emerged in the subthemes.

Sharing of information. Sharing of information emerged as a subtheme regarding internal and external exchanges of information from company employees as well as among subcontractors, suppliers, and other stakeholders. The twelve participants supported this subtheme. Participants believed that the sharing of information encouraged people to share their ideas and to share leads to some degree, which may lead to innovation. In some instances, participants received compensation for new ideas. P11 stated: "[Employees] are often told to share new ideas and are compensated when they bring new ideas to the table that helps [*sic*] improve services to the market."

Sharing information also ensures the distribution of technology in a way that the operation can continue when the manager is unavailable. Sharing of information is also an essential factor for transparency and building trust in a company and, more specifically, a working team in construction. Another aspect of sharing information was building relationships with suppliers and customers.

Bringing new ideas, processes, and technology. Bringing new ideas, processes, and technology emerged among ten participants who recognized the importance of external resources to business success, which included subcontractors, suppliers, clients, consultants, and investors. The theme of bringing new ideas, processes, and technology overlapped somewhat with the theme of sharing of information. The theme relates more to internal production line improvement. As reiterated in the literature, new ideas, processes, and technology are highly valuable vis-à-vis innovation in construction (Bergendahl and Magnusson 2015), as well as for efficient project management (Duljevic and Poturak 2017). P05, who owned a company for twenty-five years, recognized that without the skilled workers with whom he contracts for work, he would not be able to sustain his business.

P05 regretted the time he refused to integrate technology or reach out to business networks to improve his business efficiency. Often, companies in many industries resist change and technology integration out of fear of failure or because they have a negative perception of technology (Kotlar et al. 2013). Innovation is the central source of competition, yet sustaining innovation can lead to resistance (Arlbjørn and Paulraj 2013). Assuming the required people are trained to use the technology as needed, technology can ease the flow of work, increase production times, and provide room for further innovation. The level of success in implementing technological innovation depends on management practices, resources, and processes used for the implementation (Ofori-Boadu et al. 2012). The environment that enables the firm to create valuable products and services using various innovative tools determines an organization's innovation capability (Jackson et al. 2014).

Managing projects efficiently. Managing projects efficiently emerged as a subtheme from participants who described their project roles in ensuring team members completed work on time and that it was of quality. P03 improved his company's training system by issuing training tickets and by training workers on-site using technology such as a smartphone and iPad. P03 said:

> We have better oversights [*sic*] of them, and we can measure their schedules more efficiently and manage. If there are corrections that need to be made, we can do those immediately, because we see the ticket, and we're like, "Okay, there's information. We need you to go back and get

it right now, instead of having to be like a day later, "Hey, it's not on the ticket. We need to send you back."

Therefore, innovation may be required for efficient management, yet efficient management is needed for innovation. Innovation is an essential practice for the development and success of an organization (Jiménez-Jiménez and Sanz-Valle 2011; Tuan et al. 2016) and is the foundation of competitive edge (Hamdani and Wirawan 2012). The dual importance of innovation and efficient management shows the importance of training managers accurately. Abugre and Adebola (2015) added that developing and training middle managers improves their knowledge base, expectations, and personal goals.

Theme 2: Improving Competitive Performance

Participants also mentioned effective practices in improving competitive performance. Participants articulated three practices essential to success and business longevity. The literature indicated that knowledge-based corporate enterprises derive advantages from the outcome of innovations and new ideas coming from interactions between human capital and organizational structure (Salavati and Madah 2008; Saleim and Khalil 2011). The subthemes that emerged were (a) effective delivery of quality services, (b) knowledge exchange and collaboration, and (c) effective leadership.

Effective delivery of quality services. Effective delivery of quality services was the first subtheme to emerge, mentioned by the twelve participants, who maintained that services must be completed on schedule and that work be finished at minimal cost. Participants believed that quality services result in customer satisfaction, which is necessary for SMEs to remain competitive in the industry (Duljevic and Poturak 2017). Quality is a critical aspect of products and services in any industry and may lead to the retention of customers. Providing quality services and making sure customers are satisfied are ways firms can differentiate themselves from competitors (Duljevic and Poturak 2017). Consistently ensuring the effective delivery of quality services could give a construction company a competitive edge.

Knowledge exchange and collaboration. The theme of knowledge exchange and collaboration emerged during the analysis of information and resources. The transfer of information and collaboration of resources included various topical project management areas such as risk management, human resources, finances, and business strategies. Participants considered knowledge exchange and collaboration to be effective practices in management, along with learning strategic management practices to deliver projects at an appropriate cost and within a useful timeline (Tennant and Fernie 2013).

Construction companies could learn from each other and adapt their processes, which may lead to deeply seated relationships that may, in turn, lead to future business and collaboration.

Effective leadership. The theme of effective leadership emerged from various management practices mentioned by participants, including being open for collaboration, initiating and imitating new ideas, supporting ideas, embracing technology, providing incentives, mentoring, motivating, and building good rapport. Effective leadership as a theme indicated that managers succeeded as they explored effective management practices because these encompassed effective leadership strategies. Leadership is how senior leaders motivate individuals and direct them to attain goals and organizational objectives (Ofori-Boadu et al. 2012). Malcolm Baldrige National Quality Award criteria classify management practices, including aspects such as leadership (Ofori-Boadu et al. 2012). The management practices that emerged in this theme are how managers effectively lead their teams. Effective leadership was considered foundational in managing competitive construction businesses by providing vision, strategy, and direction toward achieving organizational goals (Opoku et al. 2015).

As previously mentioned, the effectiveness and efficiency of a construction company could be adversely affected if the managers appointed were not well trained and were incapable of leading a group of people. Leadership is fundamental to the construction industry and is a strategic factor in upholding sustainable practices (Opoku et al. 2015). An effective leader keeps the team positive, shares knowledge and ideas, builds trust and relationships, and creates a productive working environment; the goal is to lead to innovation in the company, which could, in turn, result in a competitive advantage. Shared understanding and trust play an important role in the construction industry (Koh and Rowlinson 2012).

Conclusions Based on the Results

Management practices in innovation in US SMEs in the construction industry involved improving project management and improving competitive performance. SME managers perceived specific valuable management practices that lead to innovation, including (a) sharing of information; (b) bringing new ideas, processes, and technology; and (c) managing projects efficiently. Additional practices are effective in managing in the competitive construction industry: (a) effective delivery of quality services, (b) knowledge exchange and collaboration, and (c) effective leadership.

Comparison of Findings with the Theoretical Framework and Previous Literature

Study findings aligned with the available literature and provided insight into the construction paradigm. Results indicated that company employees, subcontractors, suppliers, and other stakeholders shared resources in SMEs, ensuring management practices that would lead to innovation (Crema et al. 2014; Dahlander and Gann 2010). The themes and subthemes closely related to the literature: improving project management practices through (a) sharing of information, (b) bringing new ideas, processes, and technology, and (c) managing projects efficiently, and improving competitiveness through (a) effective delivery of quality services, (b) knowledge exchange and collaboration, and (c) effective leadership. Dahlander and Gann (2010) emphasized the need for companies to source, screen, assess, attain, and leverage outside knowledge resources for their own innovation practice. Similarly, Crema et al. argued that the ability of companies to create knowledge internally might not be enough. A need is growing to rely on external expertise because of limited resources (Bauer and Leker 2013; Karamanos 2015; C. Wang et al. 2014).

The first theme, improving project management, reinforces findings of previous researchers about the importance of external resources in the success of a business (Abouzeedan and Hedner 2012; Bauer and Leker 2013; Hossain 2013; Karamanos 2015; C. Wang et al. 2014). External resources are essential in any business because they can lead to success (Abouzeedan and Hedner 2012; Bauer and Leker 2013; Hossain 2013; Karamanos 2015; C. Wang et al. 2014). Similarly, an innovation culture offers workers the opportunity to generate new ideas, assess current ideas, and augment a firm's value (Bergendahl and Magnusson 2015). Consistently improving existing project management processes will lead to significant innovation.

An innovative culture calls for the willingness to experiment with new ideas, along with the ability to stimulate new ideas, develop new ways to solve problems, compensate risk-taking behaviors, and provide structural and infrastructural support to individuals and teams (Aaltonen et al. 2015; Uduma et al. 2015). In the study, one company compensated employees for bringing new ideas to improve the company services. Previous researchers also confirmed this behavior. Practices that are culturally rooted to promote positive actions among individuals in an organization could lead to successful innovation (Aaltonen et al. 2015; Brunswicker and Vanhaverbeke 2011).

Despite limited resources associated with SMEs, encouraging individuals in an organization to share new ideas freely could improve innovation (Robinson and Stubberud 2015). An upper-management innovative orientation enables organizations to generate the appropriate climate to support innovation (Kraiczy et al. 2015). What is required for innovation to be possible is difficult to determine, as the mentioned factors, themes, and subthemes interlink significantly. Leadership may be the driving force behind the practices needed consistently for innovation.

The overall theme of sharing of information was reflected in the results as a subtheme on its own but was also evident in theme 1b, bringing new ideas, processes, and technology, and in subtheme 2b: knowledge exchange and collaboration. The reiteration of sharing information indicates the importance of sharing and collaboration if one wishes to improve and move forward as a team and as a company. Learning can emerge through an organization's intranet, official group meetings, project preparation, and management in the construction industry (Tennant and Fernie 2013). The learning process starts when individuals comprehend personal experiences and learn from members of their organization (Pheng et al. 2016). By sharing knowledge and skills, organization members can learn from inside the organization. The construction industry is relatively dynamic and active in adopting new ideas and concepts from other sectors, such as value engineering and just-in-time (Pheng et al. 2016).

Interpretation of the Findings

Participants shared that they encouraged their employees to share information. Participants highlighted that they share necessary information in their external networks to serve customers. Participants mentioned the significance of collaboration with outside sources of information who can help them execute their responsibilities. A need exists to integrate internal and external sources so the company can better serve its clients (Abouzeedan and Hedner 2012; Hossain 2013; Inauen and Schenker-Wicki 2011). Internal and external exchanges of information from among company employees, as well as with subcontractors, suppliers, and other stakeholders, can be a source of innovation for the company. Sharing of information is also an essential factor for transparency and building trust in a company, and for a working team in construction.

Participants revealed that bringing new ideas, processes, and technologies was essential to creating knowledge. Participants worked with various subcontractors, suppliers, clients, consultants, and investors and used their experiences to provide an external source of expertise to the organization. Participants valued the knowledge they gleaned from external sources and believed it was able to add to or improve their current practices. Through external knowledge, new ideas emerged that could help in the innovation process of a firm (Chesbrough 2017). Results indicated that participants promoted an innovation culture, welcoming new ideas, procedures, and technology. An innovation culture in any organization would lead to the company's success, adding value to the company (Arena et al. 2017). An action is only innovative when it adds value to the existing work policies, processes, products, and services of an organization, thereby leading to an added benefit for consumers (Müller et al. 2009).

Participants who described their project roles in ensuring team members completed work projects on time and with attention to quality also identified efficient project management as important to remaining competitive in the construction industry. No reviewed studies discussed innovation in line with efficient project management. A gap in knowledge exists about efficient project management because few studies exist on project management in SMEs in the construction industry. Limited knowledge may exist because projects on SMEs in the construction industry are usually small-scale projects.

Results indicated that providing quality service is required for any organization to remain competitive, which is like the findings of Duljevic and Poturak's (2017) study. Duljevic and Poturak argued that providing quality services and making sure customers are satisfied are ways firms can differentiate themselves from competitors. They explained that customer satisfaction plays an integral part in the development of the construction management process and the development of professional–customer relationships. Customer relationships are one critical determinant of project completion and a fundamental concern of construction managers who frequently explore means to improve performance to endure in the marketplace (Duljevic and Poturak 2017).

Participants in the study confirmed that, regardless of whether the business is still operating or closed, completing services on schedule with quality finished work at a minimal cost is beneficial. In line with the effective delivery of services, participants indicated that knowledge exchange and collaboration also helps companies learn and deliver quality service to clients. Participants mentioned that shared information provides managers with better ideas for strategically managing projects at an appropriate cost and within desired timelines.

According to the results, effective leadership is fundamental if a company is to remain competitive in the construction industry. Opoku et al. (2015) reinforced this notion, stating that leadership is fundamental in the construction industry and an integral factor in upholding sustainable practices in the construction sector. Construction firms need leaders who offer collective vision, strategy, and direction toward achieving organizational goals (Opoku et al. 2015). Leadership improves innovation performance in the construction industry (Bossink 2007; Opoku et al. 2015).

Limitations

The section presents the flaws or shortcomings of the study, as well as elements that could be improved. Identifying study flaws and weaknesses may help yield stronger results in future research. In addition to the limitations, the section also presents the study delimitations. Delimitations involve things purposely not included in the study, which may be added to gain more depth and add texture to the results of future studies.

Design Limitations

Study limitations included sample size and sampling methodology. The study was limited to middle managers who had three or more years of working experience in SMEs in the construction industry. The sample was quite diverse regarding experience, yet the participants had very similar perspectives, which indicated the strength of the results. Other construction employees who do not work as middle managers may have different experiences related to management practices and innovation.

Snowball sampling as a recruiting method was a limitation because it was not possible to make inferences about the population based on the study participants. Additionally, the limited sample size may not accurately reflect the SMEs in the construction industry, even though the findings significantly related to the literature. The lack of ability to generalize the results limits the ability to make generalizable industry recommendations (Goffin et al. 2012). Study findings may be generalizable to construction companies in the United States.

The views and experiences of a novice researcher could affect how data are interpreted during the data analysis process. Biases were limited by following the data collection and data analysis procedures. The overlap in themes and participant answers may indicate that not much bias influenced the results.

The experiences of middle managers working in SMEs in the construction industry limited the results, which affected the credibility of the results. No method verified whether the information shared was accurate. Because participants' experiences and perspectives were mostly in agreement with each other and the literature, this was not a significant limitation. It was assumed that participants would share their actual experiences with management practices and innovation in the construction industry.

Delimitations

The study was delimited to management practices that could lead to innovation. Factors that promoted these management practices were not explored. Factors that served as challenges in implementing these effective management practices were intentionally not studied. The study was also delimited by the experiences and perspectives of participants in general and did not analyze the data according to the gender or length of manager experience. Also, as stated, participant responses were mostly in agreement; therefore, findings may remain consistent when controlling for demographic factors.

Implications of the Study

The study's implications are presented in two contexts: theoretical implications and practical implications. Theoretical implications involve contributions to the theory and the knowledge base of management practices and innovation involving middle managers of SMEs in construction. Practical implications include the contributions of the findings concerning their application by stakeholders in the construction industry.

Theoretical Implications

The findings from the current study contributed to OIT. Despite the growing interest in OIT research, OIT in SMEs has been inadequate in mainstream research. The abundance of studies, practices, and case studies on open innovation practices in the larger organization does not include many studies about SMEs (Rahman and Ramos 2013). SMEs have limited resources for innovation; a need exists for SMEs to collaborate with partners and networks to innovate. High wages generate scarcity of a skilled workforce, lead to a shortage of skilled resources, and lead to the purchase of a workforce because of limited economic resources (Rahman and Ramos 2013). Also, the high cost of innovation and of knowledge about open innovation strategies plays an essential part in the adoption of open innovation in SMEs.

Collaboration with other firms that aim to innovate can facilitate the exchange of knowledge, information, and experiences, thereby improving how organizations learn and work (Uduma et al. 2015). Collaboration with partners allows the exchange of explicit and tacit knowledge that facilitates the generation of innovation (Uduma et al. 2015). Results from the study showed that SMEs in the construction industry need to depend not only on internal capabilities as the source of innovation, through their employees, but also on the competencies of their innovation collaborators and networks to innovate, such as suppliers and other SMEs. OIT allows the innovation process to take place through collaboration with other organizations, entities, individuals, customers, suppliers, research laboratories, and universities to facilitate a smooth flow of ideas beyond the organization boundaries; the goal is that, in such cases, innovation drives benefits from the exploration of internal and external resources (Chesbrough 2006c).

The findings added knowledge to the existing literature on management practices by exploring the constructs of OIT to determine how middle manager practices facilitate innovations in SMEs in the construction industry. The primary constructs of OIT include collaborative innovation and innovation networks. In the current study, the link between management practices and innovation in SMEs emerged through knowledge-sharing practices, internally and externally.

Practical Implications

The results are valuable to the field of business management because SMEs have, overall, an essential part in economies. Study results could be used to improve innovation capabilities in SMEs in the construction industry through the improvement of knowledge-sharing practices internally and externally. Through the development and implementation of practices that promote innovation, SMEs can become more successful and sustainable. A need exists for additional understanding of how SMEs would survive and remain competitive because of their positive influence on the US economy and their supportive role in new employment in the marketplace.

Individuals involved in SMEs in the construction industry could use study results to address a need to collaborate with competitors, customers, suppliers, professional institutions, and research laboratories so SMEs can always implement management practices that promote innovation. Middle managers can identify and implement management practices to successfully perform responsibilities associated with innovation. The findings could help advance understanding of different management practices that can lead to real value creation, which can facilitate the growth of SMEs in the construction industry.

Those in management positions could use the findings from the study to ascertain how to promote innovation, compete, and flourish. The results could be used to inform middle managers, practitioners, and SME leaders who are considering entering innovation development. Middle managers could also use the study results to improve their understanding of middle management practices and innovation to support the sustainability of SMEs in the construction industry.

Recommendations for Further Research

The section contains recommendations for further studies. The recommendations are based on four categories that reflect the data: the data, the design, the delimitations, and issues not supported by the data.

Recommendations Developed Directly from the Data

The current study focused on middle managers in SMEs in the construction industry. Based on the data, recommendations that developed directly from the data include a more comprehensive investigation of perceived valuable management practices and innovation, and effective practices in managing the competitive construction industry. Although the data from the study contributed to the existing literature on management practices and innovation in SMEs in construction, the data may be used to explore specific elements, such as how companies share and exchange information among stakeholders in SMEs in construction. A questionnaire may be developed from the data in the study and tested using quantitative analysis to conduct a more generalizable study.

Another recommendation is to explore similarities and differences in the perspectives of construction industry SME managers regarding the differences between management and leadership, and what they believe is required from them. Because leadership is necessary for innovation, it may be interesting to analyze the responses of this population. Using a qualitative case study design would lead to truly understanding this phenomenon from various-level managers in a construction SME.

Recommendations Derived from Methodological, Research Design, or Other Limitations of the Study

Although the research purpose was to understand middle managers' experiences in SMEs in construction, the findings may not be generalizable. Recommendations derived from limitations include replicating the study with a different population and conducting the research with a quantitative or mixed design. Using a sampling method other than snowball sampling would be recommended to support any generalizations made from the sample. A quantitative or mixed design not only may help generalize study findings but also may decrease any researcher bias that may have occurred while analyzing the data. A recommendation would be to conduct a quantitative study to determine the presence of the revealed themes in SMEs in different parts of the United States as well as in various industries.

Recommendations Based on Delimitations

The current study focused on SMEs in the construction industry. Scholars could focus on SMEs in other sectors. They could concentrate on SMEs related to the construction industry, such as mining and steel firms, furniture specialists, or decorators. More knowledge about management practices of SMEs in other sectors could lead to better understanding and to development and improvement of useful methods.

Scholars could also include the perspectives of subordinates of middle managers in construction companies. Owners of construction companies could participate in further research. The new perceptions of employees and owners could provide a better understanding of effective management practices that promote innovation. Further investigation of a qualitative or quantitative nature could also explore differences found among male and female leaders in construction SMEs, as well as the differences across experience.

Recommendations to Investigate Issues Not Supported by the Data but Relevant to the Research Problem

Efficient project management was identified as a perceived valuable management practice. No current studies specifically discuss efficient project management as a management practice to promote innovation. Previous researchers focused on collaboration and integration of internal and external resources. Scholars could explore efficient project management further to determine how to develop it into a useful practice, specifically in the construction industry context.

Conclusion

Limited established management practices and innovation exist in SMEs in the construction industry (Kamal et al. 2016). Despite extensive research related to the construction industry (Shahbazpour et al. 2015; Yusof et al. 2014), scant information was available specific to management practices and innovation in SMEs in the construction industry. The current study was important in the field of business management because SMEs have an essential role in economies (Masarira and Msweli 2013) and because innovation is a primary driver in the ability of SMEs to flourish (Lee et al. 2010).

The purpose of the exploratory qualitative research study was to add to the existing literature on management practices, exploring the constructs of OIT to determine how middle manager practices facilitate innovations in SMEs in the construction industry. Based on OIT, certain practices of SMEs need to be established and enhanced to deliver products and improve processes necessary to achieve objectives and meet the needs of customers in the SME construction industry. Data collection was through semistructured interviews of twelve SME managers.

The thematic analysis results produced two themes: the perceived valuable management practices and innovation, and effective practices in managing the competitive construction industry. Results provided knowledge about how various management practices may lead to real value creation and how they may help facilitate the growth of SMEs in the construction industry. Study results could be used to improve innovation capabilities in SMEs in the construction industry through the improvement of knowledge-sharing practices, internally and externally. The study revealed valuable information for SMEs in construction and provided several avenues for future research, including the use of various methodologies and different SME industries.

REFERENCES

Aaltonen, S., A. Heinze, G. Ielpa, and D. De Tommaso. 2015. "Enterprise Cultural Heritage: The Source for Sustainable Competitive Advantage and Survival for Food Sector SMEs." *International Journal of Entrepreneurship and Innovation* 16: 73–83. https://doi.org/10.5367ijei.2015.0178.

Abouzeedan, A., and T. Hedner. 2012. "Organization Structure Theories and Open Innovation Paradigm." *World Journal of Science, Technology and Sustainable Development* 9: 6–27. https://doi.org/10.1108/20425941211223598.

Abouzeedan, A., M. Klofsten, and T. Hedner. 2013. "Internetization Management as a Facilitator for Managing Innovation in High-Technology Smaller Firms." *Global Business Review* 14: 121–36. https://doi.org/10.1177/0972150912466462.

Abreu, A., P. Macedo, and L. M. Camarinha-Matos. 2009. "Elements of a Methodology to Assess the Alignment of Core-Values in Collaborative Networks." *International Journal of Production Research* 47: 4907–34. https://doi.org/10.1080/00207540902847447.

Abugre, J. B., and K. Adebola. 2015. "An Examination of Training and Development of Middle Level Managers in Emerging Economies." *International Journal of Organizational Analysis* 23: 545–63. https://doi.org/10.1108/IJOA-10-2011-0521.

Adner, R., and R. Kapoor. 2010. "Value Creation in Innovation Ecosystems: How the Structure of Technological Interdependence Affects Firm Performance in New Technology Generations." *Strategic Management Journal* 31: 306–33. https://doi.org/10.1002/smj.821.

Adorno, M., D. Garbee, and M. L. Marix. 2016. "Advanced Literature Searches." *Clinical Nurse Specialist* 30: 141–44. https://doi.org/10.1097/NUR.0000000000000196.

Afuah, A. 2001. "Dynamic Boundaries of the Firm: Are Firms Better Off Being Vertically Integrated in the Face of a Technological Change?" *Academy of Management Journal* 44: 1211–28. https://doi.org/10.5465/3069397.

Ajayi, O. M., and S. C. Morton. 2015. "Exploring the Enablers of Organizational and Marketing Innovations in SMEs." *SAGE Open* 5 (1). Advance online publication. https://doi.org/10.1177/2158244015571487.

Akhavan, P., and A. Pezeshkan. 2014. "Knowledge Management Critical Failure Factors: A Re-Case Study." *Vine* 44: 22–41. https://doi.org/10.1108/VINE-08-2012-0034.

Alexy, O., J. Henkel, and M. W. Wallin. 2013. "From Closed to Open: Job Role Changes, Individual Predispositions, and the Adoption of Commercial Open Source Software Development." *Research Policy* 42: 1325–40. https://doi.org/10.1016/j.respol.2013.04.007.

Alhaqbani, A., D. M. Reed, B. M., Savage, and J. Ries. 2016. "The Impact of Middle Management Commitment on Improvement Initiatives in Public Organisations." *Business Process Management Journal* 22: 924–38. https://doi.org/10.1108/BPMJ-01-2016-0018.

Allwood, C. M. 2012. "The Distinction between Qualitative and Quantitative Research Methods Is Problematic." *Quality & Quantity* 46: 1417–29. https://doi.org/10.1007/s11135-011-9455-8.

al-Maian, R. Y., K. L. Needy, K. D., Walsh, and T. D. Alves. 2015. "Supplier Quality Management inside and outside the Construction Industry." *Engineering Management Journal* 27 (1): 11–22. https://doi.org/10.1080/10429247.2015.11432032.

Almirall, E., and R. Casadesus-Masanell. 2010. "Open versus Closed Innovation: A Model of Discovery and Divergence." *Academy of Management Review* 35: 27–34. https://doi.org/10.5465/AMR.2010.45577790.

Alsaawi, A. 2014. "A Critical Review of Qualitative Interviews." *European Journal of Business and Social Sciences* 3, art. 4. https://doi.org/10.2139/ssrn.2819536.

al-Sehaimi, A. O., T. F. Patricia, and L. Koskela. 2014. "Improving Construction Management Practice with the Last Planner System: A Case Study." *Engineering, Construction and Architectural Management* 21: 51–64. https://doi.org/10.1108/ECAM-03-2012-0032.

al-Shammari, H. A., and R. T. Hussein. 2007. "Strategic Planning–Firm Performance Linkage: Empirical Investigation from an Emergent Market Perspective." *Advances in Competitiveness Research* 15 (1/2): 15–26. https://www.cjournal.cz.

Andermause, R., F. K. Barg, L. Esmail, L. Edmundson, S. Girard, and A. R. Perfetti. 2017. "Qualitative Methods in Patient-Centered Outcomes Research." *Qualitative Health Research* 27: 434–42. https://doi.org/10.1177/1049732316668298.

Anderson, N., K. Potočnik, and J. Zhou. 2014. "Innovation and Creativity in Organizations: A State-of-the-Science Review, Prospective Commentary, and Guiding Framework." *Journal of Management* 40: 1297–333. https://doi.org/10.1177/0149206314527128.

Arena, M., R. Cross, J. Sims, and M. Uhl-Bien. 2017. "How to Catalyze Innovation in Your Organization." *MIT Sloan Management Review* 58 (4): 39–46. https://sloanreview.mit.edu/.

Arend, R. J. 2014. "Social and Environmental Performance at SMEs: Considering Motivations, Capabilities, and Instrumentalism." *Journal of Business Ethics* 125: 541–61. https://doi.org/10.1007/s10551-013-1934-5.

Arlbjørn, J. S., H. de Haas, and K. B. Munksgaard. 2011. "Exploring Supply Chain Innovation." *Logistics Research* 3: 3–18. https://doi.org/10.1007/s12159-010-0044-3.

Arlbjørn, J. S., and A. Paulraj. 2013. "Special Topic Forum on Innovation in Business Networks from a Supply Chain Perspective: Current Status and Opportunities for Future Research." *Journal of Supply Chain Management* 49 (4): 3–11. https://doi.org/10.1111/jscm.12034.

Asheim, B. T., and A. Isaksen. 1997. "Location, Agglomeration and Innovation: Towards Regional Innovation Systems in Norway?" *European Planning Studies* 5: 299–330. https://doi.org/10.1080/09654319708720402.

Azadegan, A. 2011. "Benefiting from Supplier Operational Innovativeness: The Influence of Supplier Evaluations and Absorptive Capacity." *Journal of Supply Chain Management* 47 (2): 49–64. https://doi.org/10.1111/j.1745-493X.2011.03226.x.

Azis, Y., M. R. Darun, D. Kartini, M. Bernik, and B. Harsanto. 2017. "A Model of Managing Innovation of SMEs in Indonesian Creative Industries." *International Journal of Business and Society* 18: 391–408. http://www.ijbs.com/.

Azis, Y., and H. Osada. 2010. "Innovation in Management System by Six Sigma: An Empirical Study of World-Class Companies." *International Journal of Lean Six Sigma* 1: 172–90. https://doi.org/10.1108/20401461011074991.

Back, C., P. A. Gustafsson, and C. Berterö. 2014. "Parental Opinions of Their Child's Experience in the Legal Process: An Interpretative Analysis." *Journal of Child Sexual Abuse* 23: 290–303. https://doi.org/10.1080/10538712.2014.888117.

Bager, T. E., K. W. Jensen, P. S. Nielsen, and T. A. Larsen. 2015. "Enrollment of SME Managers to Growth-Oriented Training Programs." *International Journal of Entrepreneurial Behavior & Research* 21: 578–99. https://doi.org/10.1108/IJEBR-12-2014-0224.

Baker, W., A. Grinstein, and N. Harmancioglu. 2016. "Whose Innovation Performance Benefits More from External Networks: Entrepreneurial or Conservative Firms?" *Journal of Product Innovation Management* 33: 104–20. https://doi.org/10.1111/jpim.12263.

Barge-Gil, A. 2010. "Cooperation-Based Innovators and Peripheral Cooperators: An Empirical Analysis of Their Characteristics and Behavior." *Technovation* 30: 195–206. https://doi.org/10.1016/j.technovation.2009.11.004.

Barrett, J. R. 2007. "The Researcher as Instrument: Learning to Conduct Qualitative Research through Analyzing and Interpreting a Choral Rehearsal." *Music Education Research* 9: 417–33. https://doi.org/10.1080/14613800701587795.

Bauer, M., and J. Leker. 2013. "Exploration and Exploitation in Product and Process Innovation the Chemical Industry." *R&D Management* 43: 196–212. https://doi.org/10.1111/radm.12012.

Baumbusch, J. 2010. "Semi-Structured Interviewing in Practice-Close Research." *Journal for Specialists in Pediatric Nursing* 15: 255–58. https://doi.org/10.1111/j.1744-6155.2010.00243.x.

Beck, E., C. Moser, and M. Tscheligi. 2014. "Memoing and Lenses: Two Approaches for Exploring Player-Generated Game Ideas in Videos." Proceedings of the 11th Conference on Advances in Computer Entertainment Technology (Art. 8). New York: ACE. https://doi.org/10.1145/2663806.2663851.

Bellucci, N. A. 2016. *A Qualitative Investigation of Strategies Used by PhD Nursing Students for Balancing Work, Family, and the Attainment of a PhD.* PhD diss., Capella University. ProQuest (UMI no. 10164291).

Bergendahl, M., and M. Magnusson. 2015. "Creating Ideas for Innovation: Effects of Organizational Distance on Knowledge Creation Processes." *Creativity & Innovation Management* 24: 87–101. https://doi.org/10.1111/caim.12097.

Birchall, J. 2014. "Qualitative Inquiry as a Method to Extract Personal Narratives: Approach to Research into Organizational Climate Change Mitigation." *Qualitative Report* 19: 1–18. https://www.nsuworks.nova.edu.

Birkinshaw, J., and P. Robbins. 2010. "Ideas at Work: Sparkling Innovation." *Business Strategy Review* 21 (2): 7–11. https://doi.org/10.1111/j.1467-8616.2010.00655.

Birks, M., Y. Chapman, and K. Francis. 2008. "Memoing in Qualitative Research: Probing Data and Processes." *Journal of Research in Nursing* 13: 68–75. https://doi.org/10.1177/1744987107081254.

Björk, J., P. Boccardelli, and M. Magnusson. 2010. "Ideation Capabilities for Continuous Innovation." *Creativity & Innovation Management* 19: 385–96. https://doi.org/10.1111/j.1467-8691.2010.00581.x.

Blank, I., L. Rokach, and G. Shani. 2016. "Leveraging Metadata to Recommend Keywords for Academic Papers." *Journal of the Association for Information Science and Technology* 67: 3073–91. https://doi.org/10.1002/asi.23571.

Bloomberg, L. D., and M. Volpe. 2008. *Completing Your Qualitative Dissertation: A Roadmap from Beginning to End.* Thousand Oaks, CA: Sage. https://doi.org/10.4135/9781452226613.

Boddy, C. R. 2016. "Sample Size for Qualitative Research." *Qualitative Market Research* 19: 426–32. https://doi.org/10.1108/QMR-06-2016-0053.

Bogers, M., A. Afuah, and B. Bastian. 2010. "Users as Innovators: A Review, Critique, and Future Research Directions." *Journal of Management* 36: 857–75. https://doi.org/10.1177/0149206309353944.

Bogers, M., and J. West. 2012. "Managing Distributed Innovation: Strategic Utilization of Open and User Innovation." *Creativity and Innovation Management* 21: 61–75. https://doi.org/10.1111/j.1467-8691.2011.00622.x.

Bogliacino, F., and M. Pianta. 2011. "Engines of Growth. Innovation and Productivity in Industry Groups." *Structural Change and Economic Dynamics* 22: 41–53. https://doi.org/10.1016/j.strueco.2010.11.002.

Bos, B. H. 2012. "Alliances and Acquisitions: A Review of Their Link to Innovation." Proceedings of the 23rd International Society for Professional Innovation Management Conference. https://www.ispim-innovation.com.

Bossink, B. A. G. 2007. "Leadership for Sustainable Innovation." *International Journal of Technology Management & Sustainable Development* 6: 135–49. https://doi.org/10.1386/ijtm.6.2.135_1.

Boudreau, K. 2010. "Open Platform Strategies and Innovation: Granting Access vs. Devolving Control." *Management Science* 56: 1849–72. https://doi.org/10.1287/mnsc.1100.1215.

Bouncken, R. B., R. Pesch, and S. Kraus. 2015. "SME Innovativeness in Buyer–Seller Alliances: Effects of Entry Timing Strategies and Inter-Organizational Learning." *Review of Managerial Science* 9: 361–84. https://doi.org/10.1007/s11846-014-0160-6.

Bourne, L., and D. H. T. Walker. 2005. "The Paradox of Project Control." *Team Performance Management* 11: 157–78. https://doi.org/10.1108/13527590510617747.

Bowen, G. A. 2010. "From Qualitative Dissertation to Quality Articles: Seven Lessons Learned." *Qualitative Report* 15: 864–79. https://www.nsuworks.nova.edu.

Braun, V., and V. Clarke. 2006. "Using Thematic Analysis in Psychology." *Qualitative Research in Psychology* 3: 77–101. https://doi.org/10.1191/1478088706qp063oa.

Brunold, J., and S. Durst. 2012. "Intellectual Capital Risks and Job Rotation." *Journal of Intellectual Capital* 13: 78–195. https://doi.org/10.1108/14691931211225021.

Brunswicker, S., and W. Vanhaverbeke. 2011. "Beyond Open Innovation in Large Enterprises: How Do Small and Medium-Sized Enterprises (SMEs) Open Up to External Innovation Sources?" *Social Science Research Network.* Advanced online publication. https://doi.org/10.2139/ssrn.1925185.

Buganza, T., D. Chiaroni, G. Colombo, and F. Frattini. 2011. "Organizational Implications of Open Innovation: An Analysis of Inter-Industry Patterns." *International Journal of Innovation Management* 15: 423–55. https://doi.org/10.1142/S1363919611003210.

Burcharth, A. L. D. A., M. P. Knudsen, and H. A. Søndergaard. 2014. "Neither Invented nor Shared Here: The Impact and Management of Attitudes for the Adoption of

Open Innovation Practices." *Technovation* 34: 149–61. https://doi.org/10.1016/j. technovation.2013.11.007.

Cachia, M., and L. Millward. 2011. "The Telephone Medium and Semi-Structured Interviews: A Complementary Fit." *Qualitative Research in Organizations and Management* 6: 265–77. https://doi.org/10.1108/17465641111188420.

Caetano, M., and D. C. Amaral. 2011. "Road Mapping for Technology Push and Partnership: A Contribution for Open Innovation Environments." *Technovation* 31: 320–35. https://doi.org/10.1016/j.technovation.2011.01.005.

Capozzi, M. M., R. Dye, and A. Howe. 2011. "Sparking Creativity in Teams: An Executive's Guide." *McKinsey Quarterly* 2: 74–81. https://www.mckinsey.com.

Caputo, M., E. Lamberti, A. Cammarano, and F. Michelino. 2016. "Exploring the Impact of Open Innovation on Firm Performances." *Management Decision* 54: 1788–812. https://doi.org/10.1108/MD-02-2015-0052.

Cassia, L., A. Colombelli, and S. Paleari. 2009. "Firms' Growth: Does the Innovation System Matter?" *Structural Change and Economic Dynamics* 20: 211–20. https://doi.org/10.1016/j.strueco.2009.01.001.

Cassiman, B., and G. Valentini. 2016. "Open Innovation: Are Inbound and Outbound Knowledge Flows Really Complementary?" *Strategic Management Journal* 37: 1034–46. https://doi.org/10.1002/smj.2375.

Cassiman, B., and R. Veugelers. 2006. "In Search of Complementarity in Innovation Strategy: Internal R&D and External Knowledge Acquisition." *Management Science* 52: 68–82. https://doi.org/10.1287/mnsc.1050.0470.

Chan, E. H. W., and R. Y. C. Tse. 2003. "Cultural Considerations in International Construction Contracts." *Journal of Construction Engineering and Management* 129: 375–81. https://doi.org/10.1061 / (ASCE) 0733-9364(2003)129:4(375).

Chen, G., G. Zhang, Y. Xie, and X. Jin. 2012. "Overview of Alliancing Research and Practice in the Construction Industry." *Architectural Engineering & Design Management* 8: 103–19. https://doi.org/10.1080/17452007.2012.659505.

Chen, P., D. Partington, and M. Qiang. 2009. "Cross-Cultural Understanding of Construction Project Managers' Conceptions of Their Work." *Journal of Construction Engineering and Management* 135: 477–87. https://doi.org/10.1061 / (ASCE) CO.1943-7862.0000009.

Chen, P., M. Qiang, and J. N. Wang. 2009. "Project Management in the Chinese Construction Industry: Six-Case Study." *Journal of Construction Engineering and Management* 135: 1016–26. https://doi.org/10.1061 / ASCE CO.1943-7862.0000067.

Chen, T. F. 2012. "Transforming Knowledge into Action to Reach Innovation Capacity in High-Tech SMEs." *International Journal of Innovation and Technology Management* 9 (1): 1–32. https://doi.org/10.1142/S0219877012500058.

Chenail, R. J. 2011. "How to Conduct Clinical Qualitative Research on the Patient's Experience." *Qualitative Report* 16: 1173–90. https://www.nsuworks.nova.edu.

Cheng, E. W., S. Kelly, and N. Ryan. 2015. "Use of Safety Management Practices for Improving Project Performance." *International Journal of Injury Control and Safety Promotion* 22: 33–39. https://doi.org/10.1080/17457300.2013.844715.

Cheng, H., F. Song, and D. Li. 2017. "How Middle Managers' Participation in Decision-Making Influences Firm Innovation Performance." *Chinese Management Studies* 11: 72–89. https://doi.org/10.1108/CMS-12-2016-0253.

Chesbrough, H. 2006a. "The Era of Open Innovation." *MIT Sloan Management Review* 44: 35–41. https://sloanreview.mit.edu/.

———. 2006b. *Open Business Models: How to Thrive in the New Innovation Landscape.* Boston: Harvard Business School Press.

———. 2006c. *Open Innovation: The New Imperative for Creating and Profiting from Technology.* Boston: Harvard Business School Press.

———. 2010. *Open Services Innovation: Rethinking Your Business to Grow and Compete in a New Era.* San Francisco: Jossey-Bass.

———. 2012. "Open Innovation: Where We've Been and Where We're Going." *Research Technology Management* 55 (4): 20–27. https://doi.org/10.5437/08956308X5504085.

———. 2017. "The Future of Open Innovation." *Research Technology Management* 60 (1): 35–38. https://doi.org/10.1080/08956308.2017.1255054.

Chesbrough, H., and S. Brunswicker. 2014. "A Fad or a Phenomenon: The Adoption of Open Innovation Practices in Large Firms." *Research Technology Management* 57 (2): 16–25. https://doi.org/10.5437/08956308X5702196.

Chesbrough, H. W., and D. J. Teece. 1996. "Organizing for Innovation." *Harvard Business Review* 74 (1): 65–73. https://hbr.org.

———. 2002. "Organizing for Innovation: When Is Virtual Virtuous?" *Harvard Business Review* 80: 335–41. https://doi.org/10.1142/9789812833181_0015.

Chiang, Y.-H., and K.-P. Hung. 2010. "Exploring Open Search Strategies and Perceived Innovation Performance from the Perspective of Inter-Organizational Knowledge Flows." *R&D Management* 40: 292–99. https://doi.org/10.1111/j.1467-9310.2010.00588.x.

Chinyamurindi, W. 2016. "Middle Manager Role and Contribution towards the Competitive Intelligence Process: A Case of Irish Subsidiaries." *South African*

Journal of Information Management 18 (2): 1–7. https://doi.org/10.4102/sajim. v18i2.727.

Chong, D. S. F., W. Eerde, C. G. Rutte, and K. H. Chai. 2012. "Bringing Employees Closer: The Effect of Proximity on Communication When Teams Function under Time Pressure: Effect of Proximity on Team Communication under Time Pressure." *Journal of Product Innovation Management* 29: 205–15. https://doi. org/10.1111/j.1540-5885.2011.00890.x.

Christensen, J. F., M. H. Olesen, and J. S. Kjaer. 2005. "The Industrial Dynamics of Open Innovation—Evidence from the Transformation of Consumer Electronics." *Research Policy* 34: 1533–49. https://doi.org/10.1016/j.respol.2005.07.002.

Clarke, V., and V. Braun. 2017. "Thematic Analysis." *Journal of Positive Psychology* 12: 297–98. https://doi.org/10.1080/17439760.2016.1262613.

Cleary, M., J. Horsfall, and M. Hayter. 2014. "Data Collection and Sampling in Qualitative Research: Does Size Matter?" *Journal of Advanced Nursing* 70: 473–75. https://doi.org/10.1111/jan.12163.

Coad, A., and R. Rao. 2008. "Innovation and Firm Growth in High-Tech Sectors: A Quantile Regression Approach." *Research Policy* 37: 633–48. https://doi. org/10.1016/j.respol.2008.01.003.

Collins, C. S., and J. E. Cooper. 2014. "Emotional Intelligence and the Qualitative Researcher." *International Journal of Qualitative Methods* 13: 88–103. https:// doi.org/10.1177/160940691401300134.

Colombo, M. G., E. Piva, and C. Rossi-Lamastra. 2014. "Open Innovation and within-Industry Diversification in Small and Medium Enterprises: The Case of Open Source Software Firms." *Research Policy* 43: 891–902. https://doi.org/10.1016/j. respol.2013.08.015.

Conboy, K., and L. Morgan. 2011. "Beyond the Customer: Opening the Agile Systems Development Process." *Information and Software Technology* 53: 535–42. https://doi.org/10.1016/j.infsof.2010.10.007.

Converse, M. 2012. "Philosophy of Phenomenology: How Understanding Aids Research." *Nurse Researcher* 20 (1): 28–32. https://doi.org/10.7748/nr2012.09.20.1.28.c9305.

Cope, R. 2014. "Salvific Significance in Personal Life Stories." *Magistra* 20 (1): 21–57. http://www.mountosb.org/publications/Magistra/subpop.html.

Coras, E. L., and A. D. Tantau. 2013. "A Risk Mitigation Model in SMEs Open Innovation Projects." *Management and Marketing* 8 (2): 303–28. https://pdfs. semanticscholar.org/8202/e802bb15bf5c5dbc1ace09097d66dadb4179.pdf?_ ga=2.51496425.1747140163.1555756463-981959867.1467672616.

Corbin, J., and A. Strauss. 2015. *Basics of Qualitative Research: Techniques and Procedures for Developing Grounded Theory.* 4th ed. Thousand Oaks, CA: Sage.

Correa, J. E. L., M. J. A. Camacho, and R. E. Mosqueda. 2015. "Application of a Model of Human Capital to Promote the Competitiveness of Small and Medium Enterprises." *Review of Business & Finance Studies* 6 (3): 31–44. https://www.theibfr.com.

Crema, M., C. Verbano, and K. Venturini. 2014. "Linking Strategy with Open Innovation and Performance in SMEs." *Measuring Business Excellence* 18 (2): 14–27. https://doi.org/10.1108/mbe-07-2013-0042.

Csath, M. 2012. "Encouraging Innovation in Small and Medium Sized Businesses: Learning Matters." *Development and Learning in Organizations* 26 (5): 9–13. https://doi.org/10.1108/14777281211258635.

Dahlander, L., and D. M. Gann. 2010. "How Open Is Innovation?" *Research Policy* 39: 699–709. https://doi.org/10.1016/j.respol.2010.01.013.

Dahlborg, C., D. Lewensohn, R. Danell, and C. J. Sundberg. 2017. "To Invent and Let Others Innovate: A Framework of Academic Patent Transfer Modes." *Journal of Technology Transfer* 42: 538–63. https://doi.org/10.1007/s10961-016-9490-7.

Davis, D. M., and J. A. Hayes. 2011. "What Are the Benefits of Mindfulness? A Practice Review of Psychotherapy-Related Research." *Psychotherapy* 48: 198–208. https://doi.org/10.1037/a0022062.

Deng, F., G. Liu, and Z. Jin. 2013. "Factors Formulating the Competitiveness of the Chinese Construction Industry: Empirical Investigation." *Journal of Management in Engineering* 29: 435–45. https://doi.org/10.1061 / (ASCE) ME.1943-5479.0000161.

Ding, G. K. C. 2008. "Sustainable Construction—the Role of Environmental Assessment Tools." *Journal of Environmental Management* 86: 451–64. https://doi.org/10.1016/j.jenvman.2006.12.025.

Dittrich, K., and G. Duysters. 2007. "Networking as a Means to Strategy Change: The Case of Open Innovation in Mobile Telephony." *Journal of Product Innovation Management* 24: 510–21. https://doi.org/10.1111/j.1540-5885.2007.00268.x.

Dowling, R., K. Lloyd, and S. Suchet-Pearson. 2016. "Qualitative Methods 1: Enriching the Interview." *Progress in Human Geography* 40: 679–86. https://doi.org/10.1177/0309132515596880.

Drew, S. A. 2006. "Building Technology Foresight: Using Scenarios to Embrace Innovation." *European Journal of Innovation Management* 9: 241–57. https://doi.org/10.1108/14601060610678121.

Du, J., B. Leten, and W. Vanhaverbeke. 2014. "Managing Open Innovation Projects with Science-Based and Market-Based Partners." *Research Policy* 43: 828–40. https://doi.org/10.1016/j.respol.2013.12.008.

Duljevic, M., and M. Poturak. 2017. "Study on Client-Satisfaction Factors in Construction Industry." *European Journal of Economic Studies* 6: 104–14. https://doi.org/10.13187/es.2017.6.104.

Duus, R., and M. Cooray. 2014. "Together We Innovate: Cross-Cultural Teamwork through Virtual Platforms." *Journal of Marketing Education* 36: 244–57. https://doi.org/10.1177./0273475314535783.

Dworkin, S. L. 2012. "Sample Size Policy for Qualitative Studies Using In-Depth Interviews." *Archives of Sexual Behavior* 41: 1319–20. https://doi.org/10.1007/s10508-012-0016-6.

Dyer, J. H. 2000. *Collaborative Advantage: Winning through Extended Enterprise Supplier Networks.* Oxford: Oxford University Press.

Eide, P., and D. Kahn. 2008. "Ethical Issues in the Qualitative Researcher–Participant Relationship." *Nursing Ethics* 15: 199–207. https://doi.org/10.1177/0969733007086018.

Engel, K., V. Dirlea, S. Dyer, and J. Graff. 2015. "Best Innovators Develop a Point of View on the Future and a Roadmap on How to Get There." *Strategy & Leadership* 43 (2): 15–22. https://doi.org/10.1108/SL-01-2015-0004.

Enkel, E., O. Gassmann, and H. Chesbrough. 2009. "Open R&D and Open Innovation: Exploring the Phenomenon." *R&D Management* 39: 311–16. https://doi.org/10.1111/j.14679310.2009.00570.

Eservel, U. Y. 2014. "IT-Enabled Knowledge Creation for Open Innovation." *Journal of the Association for Information Systems* 15: 805–34. https://doi.org/10.17705/1jais.00378.

Fleming, L., and D. M. Waguespack. 2007. "Brokerage, Boundary Spanning, and Leadership in Open Innovation Communities." *Organization Science* 18: 165–80. https://doi.org/10.1287/orsc.1060.0242.

Fu, X. 2012. "How Does Openness Affect the Importance of Incentives for Innovation?" *Research Policy* 41: 512–23. https://doi.org/10.1016/j.respol.2011.12.011.

Ganapathy, M. 2016. "Qualitative Data Analysis: Making It Easy for Nurse Researcher." *International Journal of Nursing Education* 8 (2): 106–10. https://doi.org/10.5958/0974-9357.2016.00057.X.

Gassmann, O., E. Enkel, and H. Chesbrough. 2010. "The Future of Open Innovation." *R&D Management* 40: 213–21. https://doi.org/10.1111/j.1467-9310.2010.00605.x.

Gergen, K. J., R. Josselson, and M. Freeman. 2015. "The Promises of Qualitative Inquiry." *American Psychologist* 70: 1–9. https://doi.org/10.1037/a0038597.

Gianiodis, P. T., J. E. Ettlie, and J. J. Urbina. 2014. "Open Service Innovation in the Global Banking Industry: Inside-Out versus Outside-In Strategies." *Academy of Management Perspectives* 28 (1): 76–91. https://doi.org/10.5465/amp.2012.0126.

Gilmore, A., A. McAuley, D. Gallagher, P. Massiera, and J. Gamble. 2013. "Researching SME/Entrepreneurial Research." *Journal of Research in Marketing and Entrepreneurship* 15: 87–100. https://doi.org/10.1108/jrme-10-2012-0026.

Glesne, C. 1999. *Becoming Qualitative Researchers: An Introduction.* 2nd ed. Hoboken: Pearson.

Goffin, K., J. Z. Raja, B. Claes, M. Szwejczewski, and V. Martinez. 2012. "Rigor in Qualitative Supply Chain Management Research." *International Journal of Physical Distribution & Logistics Management* 42: 804–27. https://doi.org/10.1108/09600031211269767.

Golding, J. 2009. "Data Organisation and Preparation for Statistical Analysis in a Longitudinal Birth Cohort." *Paediatric and Perinatal Epidemiology* 232 (1): 19–25. https://doi.org/10.1111/j.1365-3016.2009.01019.x.

Goodland, H., C. Lindberg, and P. Shorthouse. 2015. *Construction Innovation Project: Building BC's Vision.* https://www.bccassn.com.

Greco, M., M. Grimaldi, and L. Cricelli. 2015. "Open Innovation Actions and Innovation Performance: A Literature Review of European Empirical Evidence." *European Journal of Innovation Management* 18: 150–71. https://doi.org/10.1108/EJIM-07-2013-0074.

Grill, K. 2017. "Asymmetric Population Axiology: Deliberative Neutrality Delivered." *Philosophical Studies* 174: 219–36. https://doi.org/10.1007/s11098-016-0678-3.

———. 2009. "Search Patterns and Absorptive Capacity: Low- and High-Technology Sectors in European Countries." *Research Policy* 38: 495–506. https://doi.org/10.1016/j.respol.2008.10.006.

Grimpe, C., and W. Sofka. 2016. "Complementarities in the Search for Innovation—Managing Markets and Relationships." *Research Policy* 45: 2036–53. https://doi.org/10.1016/j.respol.2016.07.007.

Guest, G., A. Bunce, and L. Johnson. 2006. "How Many Interviews Are Enough: An Experiment with Data Saturation and Variability." *Field Methods* 18: 59–82. https://doi.org/10.1177/1525822X05279903.

Hall, B. H., and J. Lerner. 2009. *The Financing of R&D and Innovation.* Cambridge: National Bureau of Economic Research. https://doi.org/10.3386/w15325.

Hamdani, J., and C. Wirawan. 2012. "Open Innovation Implementation to Sustain Indonesian SMEs." *Procedia Economics and Finance* 4: 223–33. https://doi.org/10.1016 / s22125671(12)00337-1.

Hansen, H., and N. Trifković. 2015. "Means to an End: The Importance of the Research Question for Systematic Reviews in International Development." *European Journal of Development Research* 27: 707–26. https://doi.org/10.1057/ejdr.2014.54.

Hasan, A., and K. N. Jha. 2013. "Safety Incentive and Penalty Provisions in Indian Construction Projects and Their Impact on Safety Performance." *International Journal of Injury Control and Safety Promotion* 20: 3–12. https://doi.org/10.1080/17457300.2011.648676.

Heger, T. June. 2014. *A Theoretical Model for Networked Foresight.* Paper presented at the 25th conference of the ISPIM on Innovation for Sustainable Economy and Society, Dublin, Ireland.

Heger, T., and M. Boman. 2015. "Networked Foresight—the Case of EIT ICT Labs." *Technological Forecasting & Social Change* 101: 147–64. https://doi.org/10.1016/j.techfore.2014.02.002.

Helper, S. 2000. "Pragmatic Collaborations: Advancing Knowledge while Controlling Opportunism." *Industrial and Corporate Change* 9: 443–88. https://doi.org/10.1093/icc/9.3.443.

Hemert, P. P., P. Nijkamp, and E. Masurel. 2013. "From Innovation to Commercialisation through Networks and Agglomerations." *Annals of Regional Science* 50: 425–52. https://doi.org/10.1007/s00168-012-0509-1.

Henkel, J. 2006. "Selective Revealing in Open Innovation Processes: The Case of Embedded Linux." *Research Policy* 35: 953–69. https://doi.org/10.1016/j.respol.2006.04.010.

Herstad, S. J., C. Bloch, B. Ebersberger, and E. van de Velde. 2008. *Open Innovation and Globalisation: Theory, Evidence and Implications.* http://www.aksjonsprogrammet.no.

Herzig, S. E., and N. L. Jimmieson. 2006. "Middle Managers' Uncertainty Management during Organizational Change." *Leadership & Organization Development Journal* 27: 628–45. https://doi.org/10.1108/01437730610709264.

Hickson, I. M. 2011. "Counting to One: The Qualitative Researcher's 'Magic.'" *Journal of Occupational and Organizational Psychology* 84: 651–55. https://doi.org/10.1111/j.2044-8325.2011.02038.x.

Hilman, H., and N. Kaliappen. 2015. "Innovation Strategies and Performance: Are They Truly Linked?" *World Journal of Entrepreneurship, Management and Sustainable Development* 11: 48–63. https://doi.org/10.1108/wjemsd-04-2014-0010.

Hinde, S., and E. Spackman. 2015. "Bidirectional Citation Searching to Completion: An Exploration of Literature Searching Methods." *Pharmacoeconomics* 33: 5–11. https://doi.org/10.1007/s40273-014-0205-3.

Hossain, M. 2013. "Open Innovation: So Far and a Way Forward." *World Journal of Science, Technology and Sustainable Development* 10: 30–41. https://doi.org/10.1108/20425941311313083.

Hossain, M. 2015. "A Review of Literature on Open Innovation in Small and Medium-Sized Enterprises." *Journal of Global Entrepreneurship Research* 5 (1): 6. https://doi.org/10.1186/s40497-015-0022-y.

Housley, W., B. Dicks, K. Henwood, and R. Smith. 2017. "Qualitative Methods and Data in Digital Societies." *Qualitative Research* 17: 607–9. https://doi.org/10.1177/1468794117730936.

Huang, H.-C., M.-C. Lai, L.-H. Lin, and C.-T. Chen. 2013. "Overcoming Organizational Inertia to Strengthen Business Model Innovation." *Journal of Organizational Change Management* 26: 977–1002. https://doi.org/10.1108/JOCM-04-2012-0047.

Hughes, A. 2009. "Innovation and SMEs: Hunting the Snark—Some Reflections on the UK Experience of Support for the Small Business Sector." *Innovation: Management, Policy & Practice* 11: 114–26. https://doi.org/10.5172/impp.453.11.1.114.

Huizingh, E. K. R. E. 2011. "Open Innovation: State of the Art and Future Perspectives." *Technovation* 31: 2–9. https://doi.org/10.1016/j.technovation.2010.10.002.

Huston, L., and N. Sakkab. 2007. "Implementing Open Innovation." *Research Technology Management* 50 (2): 21–25. https://doi.org/10.1080/08956308.2007.11657426.

Ilegbinosa, I. A., and E. Jumbo. 2015. "Small and Medium Scale Enterprises and Economic Growth in Nigeria: 1975–2012." *International Journal of Business & Management* 10 (3): 203–16. https://doi.org./10.5539/ijbm.v10n3p203.

Inauen, M., and A. Schenker-Wicki. 2011. "The Impact of Outside-In Open Innovation on Innovation Performance." *European Journal of Innovation Management* 14: 496–520. https://doi.org/10.1108/14601061111174934.

Islam, M. A., M. A. Khan, A. Z. M. Obaidullah, and M. S. Alam. 2011. "Effect of Entrepreneur and Firm Characteristics on the Business Success of Small and Medium Enterprises (SMEs) in Bangladesh." *International Journal of Business & Management* 6 (3): 289–99. https://doi.org/10.5539/ijbm.v6n3p289.

Jackson, F. H., T. Sara, and S. K. Kahai. 2014. "Determinants of Innovative Capability of a Country and Its Role in Economic Growth." *International Business & Economics Research Journal* 13: 1141–47. https://doi.org10.19030/iber.v13i5.8780.

Jain, M. K., and S. K. Gandhi. 2015. "Accounting for Fixed Assets for SMEs in India vs. IFRS for SMEs: A Comparative Study and the Challenges Ahead." *International*

Journal of Multidisciplinary Approach and Studies 2 (6): 195–204. http://www.ijmas.com.

Jespersen, K. R. 2012. "Stage-to-Stage Information Dependency in the NPD Process: Effective Learning or a Potential Entrapment of NPD Gates?" *Journal of Product Innovation Management* 29: 257–74. https://doi.org/10.1111/j.1540-5885.2011.00894.x.

Jiménez-Jiménez, D., and R. Sanz-Valle. 2011. "Innovation, Organizational Learning, and Performance." *Journal of Business Research* 64: 408–17. https://doi.org/10.1016/j.jbusres.

Johansen, M., and D. P. Hawes. 2016. "The Effect of the Tasks Middle Managers Perform on Organizational Performance." *Public Administration Quarterly* 40: 589–616. https://www.paq.spaef.org.

Kahlke, R. M. 2014. "Generic Qualitative Approaches: Pitfalls and Benefits of Methodological Mixology." *International Journal of Qualitative Methods* 13: 37–52. https://doi.org/10.1177/160940691401300119.

Kallie, H., A. M. Pietila, M. Johnson, and M. Kangasniemi. 2016. "Systematic Methodological Review: Developing a Framework for a Qualitative Semi-Structured Interview Guide." *Journal of Advanced Nursing* 72: 2954–65. https://doi.org/10.1111/jan.13031.

Kamal, E. M., N. Yusof, and M. Iranmanesh. 2016. "Innovation Creation, Innovation Adoption, and Firm Characteristics in the Construction Industry." *Journal of Science & Technology Policy Management* 7: 43–57. https://doi.org/10.1108/jstpm-03-2015-0011.

Karadag, H. 2015. "Financial Management Challenges in Small and Medium-Sized Enterprises: A Strategic Management Approach." *Emerging Markets Journal* 5 (1): 26–40. https://doi.org/10.5195/emaj.2015.67.

Karamanos, A. 2015. "The Effects of Knowledge from Collaborations on the Exploitative and Exploratory Innovation Output of Greek SMEs." *Management Dynamics in the Knowledge Economy* 3: 361–80. http://www.managementdynamics.ro/.

Kazaz, A., and S. Ulubeyli. 2009. "Strategic Management Practices in Turkish Construction Firms." *Journal of Management in Engineering* 25: 185–94. https://doi.org/10.1061 / (ASCE) 0742.-597X (2009)25:4(185).

Keupp, M., and O. Gassmann. 2009. "Determinants and Archetype Users of Open Innovation." *R&D Management* 39: 331–41. https://doi.org/10.1111/j.1467-9310.2009.00563.x.

Khatun, F. 2015. "Small and Medium Enterprises (SMEs) in the Industrial Policies in Bangladesh: An Overview." *International Journal of Multidisciplinary Approach & Studies* 2 (6): 115–26. http://www.ijmas.com/.

Kim, N., D. Kim, and S. Lee. 2015. "Antecedents of Open Innovation at the Project Level: Empirical Analysis of Korean Firms." *R&D Management* 45: 411–39. https://doi.org/10.1111/radm.12088.

Kissi, J., A. Dainty, and A. Liu. 2012. "Examining Middle Managers' Influence on Innovation in Construction Professional Services Firms." *Construction Innovation* 12: 11–28. https://doi.org/10.1108/14714171211197472.

Koh, T. Y., and S. Rowlinson. 2012. "Relational Approach in Managing Construction Project Safety: A Social Capital Perspective." *Accident Analysis & Prevention* 48: 134–44. https://doi.org/10.1016/j.aap.2011.03.020.

Koskela, L., P. Tzortzopoulos, and A. al-Sehaimi. 2013. "Need for Alternative Research Approaches in Construction Management: Case Of Delay Studies." *Journal of Management in Engineering* 29: 407–13. https://doi.org/10.1061/ (ASCE) ME.1943-5479.0000148.

Koskinen, K. U. 2012. "Organizational Learning in Project-Based Companies: A Process Thinking Approach." *Project Management Journal* 43 (3): 40–49. https://doi.org/10.1002/pmj.21266.

Kotlar, J., A. De Massis, F. Frattini, M. Bianchi, and H. Fang. 2013. "Technology Acquisition in Family and Nonfamily Firms: A Longitudinal Analysis of Spanish Manufacturing Firms." *Journal of Product Innovation Management* 30: 1073–88. https://doi.org/10.1111/jpim.12046.

Kraiczy, N. D., A. Hack, and F. W. Kellermanns. 2015. "The Relationship between Top Management Team Innovation Orientation and Firm Growth: The Mediating Role of Firm Innovativeness." *International Journal of Innovation Management* 19: 1–24. https://doi.org/10.1142/S136391961550005X.

Kumar, G., and R. N. Banerjee. 2012. "Collaboration in Supply Chain." *International Journal of Productivity and Performance Management* 61: 897–918. https://doi.org/10.1108/17410401211277147.

Lam, A. 2000. "Tacit Knowledge, Organizational Learning and Societal Institutions: An Integrated Framework." *Organization Studies* 21: 487–513. https://doi.org/10.1177/0170840600213001.

Lasagni, A. 2012. "How Can External Relationships Enhance Innovation in SMEs? New Evidence for Europe." *Journal of Small Business Management* 50: 310–39. https://doi.org/10.1111/j.1540-627X.2012.00355.x.

Laursen, K., and A. J. Salter. 2014. "The Paradox of Openness: Appropriability, External Search and Collaboration." *Research Policy* 43: 867–78. https://doi.org/10.1016/j.respol.2013.10.004.

Lazonick, W. 2007. "The US Stock Market and the Governance of Innovative Enterprise." *Industrial and Corporate Change* 16: 983–1035. https://doi.org/10.1093/icc/dtm030.

Lazzarotti, V., R. Manzini, and L. Pellegrini. 2010. "Open Innovation Models Adopted in Practice: An Extensive Study in Italy." *Measuring Business Excellence* 14 (4): 11–23. https://doi.org/10.1108/13683041011093721.

Lee, S., J. Park, G. Park, and B. Yoon. 2010. "Open Innovation in SMEs: An Intermediated Network Model." *Research Policy* 39: 290–300. https://doi.org/10.1016/j.respol.2009.12.009.

Leech, N. L., and A. J. Onwuegbuzie. 2008. "Qualitative Data Analysis: A Compendium of Techniques and a Framework for Selection for School Psychology Research and Beyond." *School Psychology Quarterly* 23: 587–604. https://doi.org/10.1037/1045-3830.23.4.587.

Leedy, P. D., and J. E. Ormrod. 2010. *Practical Research: Planning and Design.* 9th ed. Hoboken: Pearson Education.

Lichtenthaler, U. 2008. "Open Innovation in Practice: An Analysis of Strategic Approaches to Technology Transactions." *IEEE Transactions on Engineering Management* 55: 148–57. https://doi.org/10.1109/TEM.2007.912932.

———. 2011. "Open Innovation: Past Research, Current Debates, and Future Directions." *Academy of Management Perspectives* 25 (1): 75–93. https://doi.org/10.5465/AMP.2011.59198451.

Lichtenthaler, U., and E. Lichtenthaler. 2009. "A Capability Based Framework for Open Innovation: Complementing Absorptive Capacity." *Journal of Management Studies* 46: 1315–38. https://doi.org/10.1111/j.1467-6486.2009.00854.x.

Locke, K. 2011. "Narratives of Quality in Qualitative Research: Putting Them in Context." *Journal of Occupational and Organizational Psychology* 84: 656–60. https://doi.org/10.1111/j.2044-8325.2011.02039.

Love, J. H., and S. Roper. 2015. "SME Innovation, Exporting and Growth: A Review of Existing Evidence." *International Small Business Journal* 33: 28–48. https://doi.org/10.1177/0266242614550190.

Mageswari, S. D. U., C. Sivasubramanian, and T. N. S. Dath. 2015. "Knowledge Management Enablers, Processes and Innovation in Small Manufacturing Firms: A Structural Equation Modeling Approach." *IUP Journal of Knowledge Management* 13 (1): 33–58. https://www.iupindia.in/default.asp.

Makui, A., P. Moeinzadeh, and M. Bagherpour. 2017. "Developing a Fuzzy Inference Approach to Evaluate the Static Complexity of Construction Projects." *Journal of Intelligent & Fuzzy Systems* 32: 2233–49. https://doi.org/10.3233/JIFS-16234.

Malmström, M., J. Wincent, and J. Johansson. 2013. "Managing Competence Acquisition and Financial Performance: An Empirical Study of How Small Firms Use Competence Acquisition Strategies." *Journal of Engineering and Technology Management* 30: 327–49. https://doi.org/10.1016/j.jengtecman.2013.07.004.

Malterud, K., V. D. Siersma, and A. D. Guassora. 2016. "Sample Size in Qualitative Interview Studies: Guided by Information Power." *Qualitative Health Research* 26: 1753–60. https://doi.org/10.1177/1049732315617444.

Manceau, D., P. Kaltenbach, L. Bagger-Hansen, V. Moatti, and J. Fabbri. 2012. "Open Innovation: Putting External Knowledge to Work." *Supply Chain Management Review* 16 (6): 42–48. https://www.scmr.com/.

Mañez, J. A., M. E. Rochina-Barrachina, A. Sanchis, and J. A. Sanchis. 2013. "Do Process Innovations Boost SMEs Productivity Growth?" *Empirical Economics* 44: 1373–405. https://doi.org/10.1007/s00181-012-0571-7.

Mann, S. 2011. "A Critical Review of Qualitative Interviews in Applied Linguistics." *Applied Linguistics* 32: 6–24. https://doi.org/10.1093/applin/amq043.

Marshall, B., P. Cardon, A. Poddar, and R. Fontenot. 2013. "Does Sample Size Matter in Qualitative Research? A Review of Qualitative Interviews in Is Research." *Journal of Computer Information Systems* 54 (1): 11–22. https://doi.org/10.1080/08874417.2013.11645667.

Masarira, S., and P. Msweli. 2013. "The Role of SMEs in National Economies: The Case of South Africa." In *Economic and Social Development: Book of Proceedings*, edited by D. Filipovic and A. G. Urnaut, 1484–94. Varazdin, Croatia: Varazdin Development and Entrepreneurship Agency.

Mason, M. 2010. "Sample Size and Saturation in Ph.D. Studies Using Qualitative Interviews." *Forum: Qualitative Social Research* 11, no. 3: art. 8. https://doi.org/10.17169/fqs-11.3.1428.

Mazzola, E., M. Bruccoleri, and G. Perrone. 2016. "Open Innovation and Firms' Performance: State of the Art and Empirical Evidences from the Biopharmaceutical Industry." *International Journal of Technology Management* 70: 109–34. https://doi.org/10.1504/IJTM.2016.075152.

McAdam, M., R. McAdam, A. Dunn, and C. McCall. 2014. "Development of Small and Medium-Sized Enterprise Horizontal Innovation Networks: UK Agri-Food Sector Study." *International Small Business Journal* 32: 830–53. https://doi.org/10.1177/0266242613476079.

Mention, A.-L. 2011. "Co-operation and Co-opetition as Open Innovation Practices in the Service Sector: Which Influence on Innovation Novelty?" *Technovation* 31: 44–53. https://doi.org/10.1016/j.technovation.2010.08.002.

Mina, A., E. Bascavusoglu-Moreau, and A. Hughes. 2014. "Open Service Innovation and the Firm's Search for External Knowledge." *Research Policy* 43: 853–66. https://doi.org/10.1016/j.respol.2013.07.004.

Mojtahed, R., M. B. Nunes, J. T. Martins, and A. Peng. 2014. "Equipping the Constructivist Researcher: The Combined Use of Semi-Structured Interviews and Decision-Making Maps." *Electronic Journal of Business Research Methods* 12: 87–95. http://www.ejbrm.com/.

Molina-Morales, F. X., and M. T. Martínez-Fernández. 2009. "Too Much Love in the Neighborhood Can Hurt: How an Excess of Intensity and Trust in Relationships May Produce Negative Effects on Firms." *Strategic Management Journal* 30 (9): 1013–23. https://doi.org/10.1002/smj.766/

Moriano, J. A., F. Molero, G. Topa, and J. P. L. Mangin. 2014. "The Influence of Transformational Leadership and Organizational Identification on Intrepreneurship." *International Entrepreneurship and Management Journal* 10: 103–19. https://doi.org/10.1007/s11365-011-0196-x.

Müller, K., C. Rammer, and J. Trüby. 2009. "The Role of Creative Industries in Industrial Innovation." *Innovation: Organization & Management* 11: 148–68. https://doi.org/10.5172/impp.11.2.148.

Najib, M., F. R. Dewi, and H. Widyastuti. 2014. "Collaborative Networks as a Source of Innovation and Sustainable Competitiveness for Small and Medium Food Processing Enterprises in Indonesia." *International Journal of Business & Management* 9: 147–60. https://doi.org/10.5539/ijbm.v9n9p147.

Oakey, R. P. 2013. "Open Innovation and Its Relevance to Industrial Research and Development: The Case of High-Technology Small Firms." *International Small Business Journal* 31: 319–36. https://doi.org/10.1177/0266242612458942.

Ofori-Boadu, A., D.-G. Owusu-Manu, D. Edwards, and G. Holt. 2012. "Exploration of Management Practices for LEED Projects." *Structural Survey* 30: 145–62. https://doi.org/10.1108/02630801211228743.

Oke, A., and A. Kach. 2012. "Linking Sourcing and Collaborative Strategies to Financial Performance. The Role of Operations Innovation." *Journal of Purchasing and Supply Management* 18: 46–59. https://doi.org/10.1016/j.pursup.2012.01.001.

Oke, A., D. Prajogo, and J. Jayaram. 2013. "Strengthening the Innovation Chain: The Role of Internal Innovation Climate and Strategic Partnerships with Supply Chain Partners." *Journal of Supply Chain Management* 49 (4): 43–58. https://doi.org/10.1111/jscm.12031.

Oke, A., F. O. Walumbwa, and A. Myers. 2012. "Innovation Strategy, Human Resource Policy, and Firms' Revenue Growth: The Roles of Environmental Uncertainty and Innovation Performance." *Decision Sciences* 43: 273–302. https://doi. org/10.1111/j.1540-5915.2011.00350.x.

Omri, W. 2015. "Innovative Behavior and Venture Performance of SMEs: The Moderating Effect of Environmental Dynamism." *European Journal of Innovation Management* 18: 195–217. https://doi.org/10.1108/EJIM-02-2013-0015.

Opoku, A., V. Ahmed, and J. Cruickshank. 2015. "Leadership Style of Sustainability Professionals in the UK Construction Industry." *Built Environment Project and Asset Management* 5: 184–201. https://doi.org/10.1108/BEPAM-12-2013-0075.

Othman Idrissia, M., N. Amaraa, and R. Landrya. 2012. "SMEs' Degree of Openness: The Case of Manufacturing Industries." *Journal of Technology Management & Innovation* 7 (1): 186–210. https://doi.org/10.4067/S0718-27242012000100013.

Page, A. L., and G. R. Schirr. 2008. "Growth and Development of a Body of Knowledge: 16 Years of New Product Development Research, 1989–2004." *Journal of Product Innovation Management* 25: 233–48. https://doi. org/10.1111/j.1540-5885.2008.00297.x.

Pajares, F. 2007. "Empirical Properties of a Scale to Assess Writing Self-Efficacy in School Contexts." *Measurement and Evaluation in Counseling and Development* 39: 239–49. https://doi.org/10.1080/07481756.2007.11909801.

Parasuraman, A. 2000. "Technology Readiness Index (TRI), a Multiple-Item Scale to Measure Readiness to Embrace New Technologies." *Journal of Service Research* 2: 307–20. https://doi.org/10.1177/109467050024001.

Parida, V., M. Westerberg, and J. Frishammar. 2012. "Inbound Open Innovation Activities in High-Tech SMEs: The Impact on Innovation Performance." *Journal of Small Business Management* 50: 283–309. https://doi. org/10.1111/j.1540-627X.2012.00354.x.

Paunov, C. 2012. "The Global Crisis and Firms' Investments in Innovation." *Research Policy* 41: 24–35. https://doi.org/10.1016/j.respol.2011.07.007.

Percy, W. H., K. Kostere, and S. Kostere. 2015. "Generic Qualitative Research in Psychology." *Qualitative Report* 20: 76–85. https://www.nsuworks.nova.edu/.

Perez, P. B., M. C. González-Cruz, and J. P. Pastor-Ferrando. 2010. "Analysis of Construction Projects by Means of Value Curves." *International Journal of Project Management* 28: 719–31. https://doi.org/10.1016/j.ijproman.2009.11.003.

Peters, K., and E. Halcomb. 2015. "Interviews in Qualitative Research." *Nurse Researcher* 22 (4): 6–7. https://doi.org/10.7748/nr.22.4.6.s2.

Petrariu, I. R., R. Bumbac, and R. Ciobanu. 2013. "Innovation: A Path to Competitiveness and Economic Growth. The Case of CEE Countries." *Theoretical and Applied Economics* 5 (582): 15–26. http://www.ectap.ro/.

Phelps, C. C. 2010. "A Longitudinal Study of the Influence of Alliance Network Structure and Composition on Firm Exploratory Innovation." *Academy of Management Journal* 53: 890–913. https://doi.org/10.5465/AMJ.2010.52814627.

Pheng, L. S., G. Shang, and W. K. Foong. 2016. "Enhancing Construction Productivity through Organizational Learning in the Singapore Construction Industry." *International Journal of Construction Project Management* 8: 71–89. https://www.iaeme.com/IJCE/index.asp.

Philip, M. 2011. "Factors Affecting Business Success of Small and Medium Enterprises (SMEs)." *Amity Global Business Review* 6 (1): 118–36. http://www.amity.edu/aibs/aibs_journals.asp.

Piore, M., and C. Sabel. 1984. *The Second Industrial Divide: Prospects for Prosperity.* New York: Basic Books.

Pisano, G. P. 2015. "You Need an Innovation Strategy." *Harvard Business Review* 93 (6): 44–54. https://www.hbr.org.

Pisano, G. P., and R. Verganti. 2008. "Which Kind of Collaboration Is Right for You?" *Harvard Business Review* 86 (12): 78–86. https://www.hbr.org.

Powell, M. B., C. H. Hughes-Scholes, C. Cavezza, and M. A. Stoové. 2010. "Examination of the Stability and Consistency of Investigative Interviewer Performance across Similar Mock Interview Contexts." *Legal and Criminological Psychology* 15: 243–60. https://doi.org/10.1348/135532509X472077.

Pullen, A. J. J., P. C. de Weerd-Nederhof, A. J. Groen, and O. A. M. Fisscher. 2012. "Open Innovation in Practice: Goal Complementarity and Closed NPD Networks to Explain Differences in Innovation Performance for SMEs in the Medical Devices Sector." *Journal of Product Innovation Management* 29: 917–34. https://doi.org/10.1111/j.1540-5885.2012.00973.x.

Rahman, H., and I. Ramos. 2013. "Challenges in Adopting Open Innovation Strategies in SMEs: An Exploratory Study in Portugal." *Issues in Informing Science and Information Technology* 10: 431–48. https://doi.org/10.28945/1820.

Rampersad, G., P. Quester, and I. Troshani. 2010. "Managing Innovation Networks: Exploratory Evidence from ICT, Biotechnology and Nanotechnology Networks." *Industrial Marketing Management* 39: 793–805. https://doi.org/10.1016/j.indmarman.2009.07.002.

Randhawa, K., R. Wilden, and J. Hohberger. 2016. "A Bibliometric Review of Open Innovation: Setting a Research Agenda." *Journal of Product Innovation Management* 33: 750–72. https://doi.org/10.1111/jpim.12312.

Rangus, K. 2017. "Does a Firm's Open Innovation Mode Matter?" *Economic and Business Review for Central and South-Eastern Europe* 19 (2): 181–201, 269. https://doi.org/10.15458/85451.45.

Ren, S., L. Wang, W. Yang, and F. Wei. 2013. "The Effect of External Network Competence and Intrafirm Networks on a Firm's Innovation Performance: The Moderating Influence of Relational Governance." *Innovation: Management, Policy & Practice* 15: 17–34. https://doi.org/10.5172/impp.2013.15.1.17.

Robinson, S., and H. A. Stubberud. 2015. "A Comparison of Methods of Creativity in Small and Large European Businesses." *International Journal of Entrepreneurship* 19: 140–51. https://www.abacademies.org/journals/international-journal-of-entrepreneurship-home.html.

Rodríguez-Ferradas, M. I., and J. A. Alfaro-Tanco. 2016. "Open Innovation in Automotive SMEs Suppliers: An Opportunity for New Product Development." *Universia Business Review* 50: 142–57. https://doi.org/10.3232/UBR.2016.V13.N2.05.

Rogbeer, S., R. Almahendra, and B. Ambos. 2014. "Open-Innovation Effectiveness: When Does the Macro Design of Alliance Portfolios Matter?" *Journal of International Management* 20: 464–77. https://doi.org/10.1016/j.intman.2014.09.003.

Rohrbeck, R., K. Hölzle, and H. G. Gemünden. 2009. "Opening Up for Competitive Advantage—How Deutsche Telekom Creates an Open Innovation Ecosystem." *R&D Management* 39: 420–30. https://doi.org/10.1111/j.1467-9310.2009.00568.x.

Ross, M. W., M. Y. Iguchi, and S. Panicker. 2018. "Ethical Aspects of Data Sharing and Research Participant Protections." *American Psychologist* 73: 138–45. https://doi.org/10.1037/amp0000240.

Roussel, P. A., K. N. Saad, and T. J. Erickson. 1991. *Third Generation R & D: Managing the Link to Corporate Strategy.* Boston: Harvard Business School Press.

Saguy, S. I. 2011. "Academia-Industry Innovation Interaction: Paradigm Shifts and Avenues for the Future." *Procedia Food Science* 1: 1875–82. https://doi.org/10.1016/j.profoo.2011.09.275.

Saini, R. 2015. "Linking Knowledge Management and Innovation in SMEs: A Structural Equation Modeling Approach." *IUP Journal of Knowledge Management* 13 (2): 45–64. https://www.iupindia.in/default.asp.

Salavati, S. B., and M. Madah. 2008. "Knowledge Capital Reporting in Knowledge Based Enterprises Using the Arc Model." *Roshd-e-fanavari* 4 (15): 41–47. http://www.roshdefanavari.ir/En/.

Saldaña, J. 2009. "Popular Film as an Instructional Strategy in Qualitative Research Methods Courses." *Qualitative Inquiry* 15: 247–61. https://doi.org/10.1177/1077800408318323.

Saleim, A. A. S., and O. E. M. Khalil. 2011. "Understanding the Knowledge Management-Intellectual Capital Relationship: A Two-Way Analysis." *Journal of Intellectual Capital* 12: 586–614. https://doi.org/10.1108/14691931111181742.

Salih, A., and Y. Doll. 2013. "A Middle Management Perspective on Strategy Implementation." *International Journal of Business & Management* 8 (22): 32–39. https://doi.org/10.5539/ijbm.v8n22p32.

Sandelowski, M. 2000. "Whatever Happened to Qualitative Description?" *Research in Nursing & Health* 23: 334–40. https://doi.org/10.1002/1098-240X / (200008)23:4<334: AID-NUR9>3.0.CO; 2-G.

———. "A Matter of Taste: Evaluating the Quality of Qualitative Research." *Nursing Inquiry* 22: 86–94. https://doi.org/10.1111/nin.12080.

Santos-Vijande, M. L., J. Á. López-Sánchez, and J. A. Trespalacios. 2012. "How Organizational Learning Affects a Firm's Flexibility, Competitive Strategy, and Performance." *Journal of Business Research* 65: 1079–89. https://doi.org/10.1016/j.jbusres.2011.09.002.

Sargeant, J. 2012. "Qualitative Research Part II: Participants, Analysis, and Quality Assurance." *Journal of Graduate Medical Education* 4: 1–3. https://doi.org/10.4300/jgme-d-11-00307.1.

Saunila, M., J. Ukko, and H. Rantanen. 2014. "Does Innovation Capability Really Matter for the Profitability of SMEs? Innovation Capability and Profitability in SMEs." *Knowledge and Process Management* 21: 134–42. https://doi.org/10.1002/kpm.1442.

Schlagwein, D., K. Conboy, J. Feller, J. M. Leimeister, and L. Morgan. 2017. "'Openness' with and without Information Technology: A Framework and a Brief History." *Journal of Information Technology* 32: 297–305. https://doi.org/10.1057/s41265-017-0049-3.

Seers, K. 2012. "Qualitative Data Analysis." *Evidence-Based Nursing* 15: 2. https://doi.org/10.1136/ebnurs.2011.100352.

Segerstedt, A., and T. Olofsson. 2010. "Supply Chains in the Construction Industry." *Supply Chain Management* 15: 347–53. https://doi.org/10.1108/13598541011068260.

Sev, A. 2009. "How Can the Construction Industry Contribute to Sustainable Development? A Conceptual Framework." *Sustainable Development* 17: 161–73. https://doi.org/10.1002/sd.373.

Shah, P. K., C. Perez-Iratxeta, P. Bork, and M. A. Andrade. 2003. "Information Extraction from Full Text Scientific Articles: Where Are the Keywords?" *BMC Bioinformatics* 4, art. 20. https://doi.org/10.1186/1471-2105-4-20.

Shahbazpour, M., M. Noktehdan, and S. Wilkinson. June 2015. "Innovation Classification and Measurement System for Construction Industry." Paper presented at the 26th ISPIM Conference: Shaping the Frontiers of Innovation Management, Budapest, Hungary. https://www.innoget.com.

Soltanifar, E., and M. Ansari. 2016. "Matrix-Collage: An Innovative Methodology for Qualitative Inquiry in Social Systems." *Electronic Journal of Business Research Methods* 14: 8–27. http://www.ejbrm.com/main.html.

Sorescu, A. B., and J. Spanjol. 2008. "Innovation's Effect on Firm Value and Risk: Insights from Consumer Packaged Goods." *Journal of Marketing* 72 (2): 114–32. https://doi.org/10.1509/jmkg.72.2.114.

Spithoven, A., B. Clarysse, and M. Knockaert. 2011. "Building Absorptive Capacity to Organise Inbound Open Innovation in Traditional Industries." *Technovation* 31: 10–21. https://doi.org/10.1016/j.technovation.2010.10.003.

Spithoven, A., W. Vanhaverbeke, and N. Roijakkers. 2013. "Open Innovation Practices in SMEs and Large Enterprises." *Small Business Economics* 41: 537–62. https://doi.org/10.1007/s11187-012-9453-9.

Standing, C., and S. Kiniti. 2011. "How Can Organizations Use Wikis for Innovation?" *Technovation* 31: 287–95. https://doi.org/10.1016/j.technovation.2011.02.005.

Stanislawski, R., and R. Lisowski. 2015. "The Relations between Innovation Openness (Open Innovation) and the Innovation Potential of SMEs." *Procedia Economics and Finance* 23: 1521–26. https://doi.org/10.1016 / S2212-5671(15)00330-5.

Storchevoi, M. A. 2015. "The Theory of the Firm and Strategic Management." *Problems of Economic Transition* 57 (9): 1–19. https://doi.org/10.1080/10611991.2014.1 088357.

Story, V. M., N. Boso, and J. W. Cadogan. 2015. "The Form of Relationship between Firm-Level Product Innovativeness and New Product Performance in Developed and Emerging Markets." *Journal of Product Innovation Management* 32: 45–64. https://doi.org/10.1111/jpim.12180.

Stroh, P. J. 2015. "Advancing Innovation: What's Your Role? Adding Discipline and Execution to the Mix of Creativity and Ideation Will Help You and Your Company Succeed." *Strategic Finance* 97 (3): 24–32. https://www.sfmagazine.com/.

Su, Y., P. Hsu, and N. Pai. 2010. "An Approach to Discover and Recommend Cross-Domain Bridge-Keywords in Document Banks." *Electronic Library* 28: 669–87. https://doi.org/10.1108/02640471011081951.

Suh, Y., and M. Kim. 2012. "Effects of SME Collaboration on R&D in the Service Sector in Open Innovation." *Innovation* 14: 349–62. https://doi.org/10.5172/impp.2012.14.3.349.

Sutton, J., and Z. Austin. 2015. "Qualitative Research: Data Collection, Analyses, & Management." *Canadian Journal of Hospital Pharmacy* 68: 226–31. https://doi.org/10.4212/cjhp.v68i3.1456.

Szczepańska-Woszczyna, K. 2014. "SMEs Managers—a Need for Competence." *Acta Technologica Dubnicae* 4 (1): 1–16. https://doi.org/10.1515/atd-2015-0008.

Talegeta, S. 2014. "Innovation and Barriers to Innovation: Small and Medium Enterprises in Addis Ababa." *Journal of Small Business and Entrepreneurship Development* 2 (1): 83–106. http://www.jsbednet.com.

Tapscott, D., and A. D. Williams. 2006. *Wikinomics: How Mass Collaboration Changes Everything.* New York: Portfolio.

Tenenberg, J. 2014. "Asking Research Questions: Theoretical Presuppositions." *ACM Transactions on Computing Education* 14, no. 3: art. 16. https://doi.org/10.1145/2644924.

Tennant, S., and S. Fernie. 2013. "Organizational Learning in Construction Supply Chains." *Engineering, Construction and Architectural Management* 20: 83–98. https://doi.org/10.1108/09699981311288691.

Theyel, N. 2013. "Extending Open Innovation throughout the Value Chain by Small and Medium-Sized Manufacturers." *International Small Business Journal* 31: 256–74. https://doi.org/10.1177/0266242612458517.

Thomas, D. R. 2006. "A General Inductive Approach for Analyzing Qualitative Evaluation Data." *American Journal of Evaluation* 27: 237–46. https://doi.org/10.1177/1098214005283748.

Thompson, S. 2017. "Qualitative Methods and Public Policy." *Journal of Positive Psychology* 12: 321–22. https://doi.org/10.1080/17439760.2016.1262623.

Török, A., and J. Tóth. 2013. "Open Characters of Innovation Management in the Hungarian Wine Industry." *Agricultural Economics* 59: 430–38. https://doi.org/10.17221/24/2013-AGRICECON.

Tracy, S. J. 2010. "Qualitative Quality: Eight 'Big-Tent' Criteria for Excellent Qualitative Research." *Qualitative Inquiry* 16: 837–51. https://doi.org/10.1177/1077800410383121.

Trott, P., and P. Hartmann. 2009. "Why 'Open Innovation' Is Old Wine in New Bottles." *International Journal of Innovation Management* 13: 715–30. https://doi.org/10.1142/S1363919609002509.

Tuan, N., N. Nhan, P. Giang, and N. Ngoc. 2016. "The Effects of Innovation on Firm Performance of Supporting Industries in Hanoi, Vietnam." *Journal of Industrial Engineering and Management* 9: 413–31. https://doi.org/10.3926/jiem.1564.

Tucci, C. L., H. Chesbrough, F. Piller, and J. West. 2016. "When Do Firms Undertake Open, Collaborative Activities? Introduction to the Special Section on Open Innovation and Open Business Models." *Industrial and Corporate Change* 25: 283–88. https://doi.org/10.1093/icc/dtw002.

Tufford, L., and P. Newman. 2010. "Bracketing in Qualitative Research." *Qualitative Social Work* 11: 80–96. https://doi.org/10.1177/1473325010368316.

Tzortzaki, A. M., and A. Mihiotis. 2014. "A Review of Knowledge Management Theory and Future Directions." *Knowledge and Process Management* 21: 29–41. https://doi.org/10.1002/kpm.1429.

Uduma, I. A., A. F. Wali, and L. T. Wright. 2015. "A Quantitative Study on the Influence of Breadth of Open Innovation on SMEs Product-Service Performance: The Moderating Effect of Type of Innovation." *Cogent Business & Management* 2, art. 120421. https://doi.org/10.1080/23311975.2015.1120421.

US Department of Health and Human Services, National Commission for the Protection of Human Subjects of Biomedical and Behavioral Research. 1979. *The Belmont Report: Ethical Principles and Guidelines for the Protection of Human Subjects of Research* (45 CFR 46). http://www.hhs.gov/ohrp/regulations-and-policy/belmont-report/.

Van den Bossche, P., M. Segers, and N. Jansen. 2010. "Transfer of Training: The Role of Feedback in Supportive Social Networks." *International Journal of Training and Development* 14: 81–94. https://doi.org/10.1111/j.1468-2419.2010.00343.x.

van de Vrande, V., J. P. J. de Jong, W. Vanhaverbeke, and M. de Rochemont. 2009. "Open Innovation in SMEs: Trends, Motives and Management Challenges." *Technovation* 29: 423–37. https://doi.org/10.1016/j.technovation.2008.10.001.

van de Vrande, V., C. Lemmens, and W. Vanhaverbeke. 2006. "Choosing Governance Modes for External Technology Sourcing." *R&D Management* 36: 347–63. https://doi.org/10.1111/j.1467-9310.2006.00434.x.

Vanhaverbeke, W. 2013. "Rethinking Open Innovation beyond the Innovation Funnel." *Technology Innovation Management Review* 3 (4): 6–10. https://www.timreview.ca.

Vanhaverbeke, W. P. M., and M. M. A. H. Cloodt. 2006. "Open Innovation in Value Networks." In *Open Innovation: Researching a New Paradigm*, edited by H. Chesbrough and W. Vanhaverbeke, 258–81. Oxford: Oxford University Press.

Vanhoucke, M. 2011. "On the Dynamic Use of Project Performance and Schedule Risk Information during Project Tracking." *Omega* 39: 416–26. https://doi.org/10.1016/j.omega.2010.09.006.

Waas, T., A. Verbruggen, and T. Wright. 2010. "University Research for Sustainable Development: Definition and Characteristics Explored." *Journal of Cleaner Production* 18: 629–36. https://doi.org/10.1016/j.jclepro.2009.09.017.

Wagner, S. 2012. "Tapping Supplier Innovation." *Journal of Supply Chain Management* 48 (2): 37–52. https://doi.org/10.1111/j.1745-493X.2011.03258.x.

Wang, C., S. Rodan, M. Fruin, and X. Xu. 2014. "Knowledge Networks, Collaboration Networks, and Exploratory Innovation." *Academy of Management Journal* 57: 454–514. https://doi.org/10.5465/amj.2011.0917.

Wang, K. Y., A. Hermens, K. Huang, and J. Chelliah. 2015. "Entrepreneurial Orientation and Organizational Learning on SMEs' Innovation." *International Journal of Organizational Innovation* 7 (4): 71–81. http://www.ijoi-online.org/index.php.

West, J. 2014. "Challenges of Funding Open Innovation Platforms." In *New Frontiers in Open Innovation*, edited by H. Chesbrough, W. Vanhaverbeke, and J. West, 22–49. https://doi.org/10.1093/acprof:oso/9780199682461.003.0004.

West, J., and M. Bogers. 2014. "Leveraging External Sources of Innovation: A Review of Research on Open Innovation." *Journal of Product Innovation Management* 31: 814–31. https://doi.org/10.1111/jpim.12125.

———. 2017. Open Innovation: Current Status and Research Opportunities." *Innovation: Organization & Management* 19: 43–50. https://doi.org/10.1080/14479338.2016.1258995.

West, J., and K. R. Lakhani. 2008. "Getting Clear about Communities in Open Innovation." *Industry and Innovation* 15: 223–31. https://doi.org/10.1080/13662710802033734.

West, J., A. Salter, W. Vanhaverbeke, and H. Chesbrough. 2014. "Open Innovation: The Next Decade." *Research Policy* 43: 805–11. https://doi.org/10.1016/j.respol.2014.03.001.

Whittaker, D. H., B. P. Fath, and A. Fiedler. 2016. "Assembling Capabilities for Innovation: Evidence from New Zealand SMEs." *International Small Business Journal* 34: 123–43. https://doi.org/10.1016/j.procs.2016.07.060.

Wonglimpiyarat, J. 2015. "Challenges of SMEs Innovation and Entrepreneurial Financing." *World Journal of Entrepreneurship, Management and Sustainable Development* 11: 295–311. https://doi.org/10.1108/wjemsd-04-2015-0019.

Wright, T. 2014. "Gender, Sexuality and Male-Dominated Work: The Intersection of Long-Hours Working and Domestic Life." *Work, Employment and Society* 28: 985–1002. https://doi.org/10.1177/0950017013512713.

Wynarczyk, P. 2013. "Open Innovation in SMEs." *Journal of Small Business and Enterprise Development* 20: 258–78. https://doi.org/10.1108/14626001311326725.

Xiaobao, P., S. Wei, and D. Yuzhen. 2013. "Framework of Open Innovation in SMEs in an Emerging Economy: Firm Characteristics, Network Openness, and Network Information." *International Journal of Technology Management* 62: 223–50. https://doi.org/10.1504/IJTM.2013.055142.

Ybarra, M. L., T. L. Prescott, G. L. Phillips, J. T. Parsons, S. S. Bull, and B. Mustanski. 2016. "Ethical Considerations in Recruiting Online and Implementing a Text Messaging–Based HIV Prevention Program with Gay, Bisexual, and Queer Adolescent Males." *Journal of Adolescent Health* 59: 44–49. https://doi.org/10.1016/j.jadohealth.2016.03.020.

Yin, R. K. 2011. *Qualitative Research from Start to Finish.* New York: Guilford Press.

Yoo, S., O. Sawyerr, and W. Tan. 2015. "The Impact of Exogenous and Endogenous Factors on External Knowledge Sourcing for Innovation: The Dual Effects of the External Environment." *Journal of High Technology Management Research* 26: 14–26. https://doi.org/10.1016/j.hitech.2015.04.002.

Yun, J. H. J., and A. V. Mohan. 2012. "Exploring Open Innovation Approaches Adopted by Small and Medium Firms in Emerging/Growth Industries: Case Studies from Daegu–Gyeongbuk Region of South Korea." *International Journal of Technology, Policy and Management* 12 (1): 1–19. https://doi.org/10.1504/IJTPM.2012.044965.

Yusof, N. A., and N. Z. Abidin. 2011. "Does Organizational Culture Influence the Innovativeness of Public-Listed Housing Developers?" *American Journal of Applied Sciences* 8: 724–35. https://doi.org/10.3844/ajassp.2011.724.735.

Yusof, N., E. Mustafa Kamal, L. Kong-Seng, and M. Iranmanesh. 2014. "Are Innovations Being Created or Adopted in the Construction Industry? Exploring Innovation in the Construction Industry." *Sage Open* 4, no. 3. Advanced online publication. https://doi.org/10.1177/2158244014552424.

Zakaria, N., N. A. Chew-Abdullah, and R. Z. Yusoff. 2016. "Empirical Review on Innovation-Performance Linkage in Malaysian Manufacturing SMEs." *International Review of Management and Marketing* 6 (7) 101–6. http://www.econjournals.com/index.php/index/index.

Zeng, S. X., X. M. Xie, and C. M. Tam. 2010. "Relationship between Cooperation Networks and Innovation Performance of SMEs." *Technovation* 30: 181–94. https://doi.org/10.1016/j.technovation.2009.08.003.

Zhou, K. Z., and C. B. Li. 2012. "How Knowledge Affects Radical Innovation: Knowledge Base, Market Knowledge Acquisition, and Internal Knowledge Sharing." *Strategic Management Journal* 33: 1090–1102. https://doi.org/10.1002/smj.1959.

Zitomer, M. R., and D. Goodwin. 2014. "Gauging the Quality of Qualitative Research in Adapted Physical Activity." *Adapted Physical Activity Quarterly* 31: 193–218. https://doi.org/10.1123/apaq.2013-0084.

Printed in the United States
By Bookmasters